HAUS CURIOSITIES

Trust in Public Life

About the Contributors

Claire Gilbert is the founder director of the Westminster Abbey Institute. A current and former member of numerous ethics committees, Dr Gilbert has played an instrumental role in the medical research ethics field, and has led efforts to shift the Church's thinking on environmental issues.

Josie Rourke is a theatre and film director and formerly the artistic director of the Bush Theatre (2007–11) and the Donmar Warehouse (2012–19). In 2018 Rourke made her feature-film debut with the Academy Award- and BAFTA-nominated film *Mary Queen of Scots*.

Anthony Ball is canon rector at Westminster Abbey and an assistant bishop in the Anglican diocese of Egypt. As a former member of the Diplomatic Service, he has been posted overseas in the Middle East and Spain, during which time he was ordained as a priest. He subsequently had roles in Lambeth Palace, school chaplaincy, and parish ministry.

James Hawkey is canon theologian of Westminster Abbey, a chaplain to King Charles III, and chair of the Westminster Abbey Institute. Canon Hawkey is also a bye-fellow of Clare College, Cambridge, and holds visiting professorships in theology at King's College, London, and the Pontificia Università Gregoriana in Rome.

Anna Rowlands is St Hilda professor of Catholic social thought and practice in the Department of Theology and Religion at the University of Durham.

TRUST IN PUBLIC LIFE

Edited and with an introduction by Claire Gilbert

First published by Haus Publishing in 2023
4 Cinnamon Row
London SW11 3TW
www.hauspublishing.com

A CIP catalogue record for this book is
available from the British Library

Print ISBN: 978-1-913368-75-3
Ebook ISBN: 978-1-913368-76-0

Typeset in Garamond by MacGuru Ltd

Printed in Czechia

Contents

Introduction   1
Claire Gilbert

Trust in Oneself   5
Claire Gilbert

Trust in Oneself: A Response   25
Josie Rourke

Trust in Institutions   35
Anthony Ball

Trust in People   57
James Hawkey

The Roots of Trust   81
Anna Rowlands

Notes   105

Introduction

Claire Gilbert

A former cabinet minister told me that whenever he was in post and under fire for some perceived government misdemeanour, the trick was not to ignore the criticism and anger, nor simply to apologise, but to come to Parliament and explain, *in minute detail*, what had happened and why. He said that in this way, there would be no lies told, no responsibility evaded, but everyone listening would become lost in the detail, bored by the monologue, and the anger would dissipate. A clever method and on the face of it laudable: but is the heart of the matter drowned in an ocean of words? And although this is undoubtedly transparency, does it restore trust?

Onora O'Neill, whose famous 2002 Reith Lectures are cited several times in this book, did not think so. As Anna Rowlands observes, it is a reduction in deception and lies rather than a reduction in (mere) secrecy that is needed. In her essay, 'The Roots of Trust', Rowlands argues that the erosion of our trust in public figures and institutions is a specific feature of modernity, by which our lonely and sceptical selves fly solo. Artificial, abstract policies and procedures will not increase trust, according to Rowlands. It will only grow by means of actual encounters with real people and multiple loving acts of committed entrustment. James Hawkey agrees – trust can't be injected like a vaccine, he writes in his essay 'Trust in People'. To trust is to risk, to become vulnerable, to place the centre of our universe somewhere other than ourselves. This is the challenge of our age: to incubate trust, solidarity, and truthfulness as habits that do not need to be defended. Anthony Ball, in 'Trust in Institutions', makes a case for the institutional and individual habits that must be inculcated to do this: being honest with an intelligent, not an indiscriminate, openness; having the humility to question whether one's institution is offering the right answers or addressing the needs of the public; manifesting compassion – people trust those with whom they have most contact, the front-line staff, far more than faceless bureaucracies; and being competent. These virtues need commitment and to be energetically cultivated, as in the hard work of a gardener, to generate trust.

Trust in oneself, in institutions, and in each other is an activity, not a state. Perfection is not, and could not, be the goal. In my essay, 'Trust in Oneself', and Josie Rourke's response we use the characters of Shakespeare's

Measure for Measure to argue for the courage, the act of trust, to walk towards the uncertainty of self-knowledge and learn self-trust there, in the fallible mix of good and bad that humans are. Trust is to be found in the flickering light of the attempt to live well, which usually fails, says Rowlands. Hawkey urges a 'gratuitous' solidarity that sustains trust amid flux and disagreement. Transactional solidarity will not do this. As with the virtues espoused by Ball, these are not visions of utopia but endeavours, made among and with each other.

The essays in this book are edited versions of lectures given in Westminster Abbey in the spring of 2022. Together they provide deep reflections on the nature of trust in the context of public life, agreeing that it cannot be engendered in the abstract or by force, but only through real encounters. They offer guidance on how to make those encounters generative of lasting trust, whether they be within oneself, between people, or within institutions and among the people they serve. 'It is our responsibility to face the troubling and difficult things within our problem selves,' Rourke writes. 'And to move forward in the hope of a more honest and compassionate life, self, and – perhaps – story.'

Trust in Oneself

Claire Gilbert

This essay and Josie Rourke's response use the play *Measure for Measure* by William Shakespeare as a guide. The wisdom drawn from the play does not depend upon you knowing it, but for clarity, the plot can be summarised thus. It is set in the city-state of Vienna. Duke Vincentio, who rules the city, has decided to withdraw from public office because he has not successfully enforced the city's strict laws and thinks he does not have the strength of will to do so. In his place he appoints Angelo, who is ascetic, chaste, self-disciplined, and iron-willed. As governor, Angelo enforces the law mercilessly: the brothels are closed and extramarital fornication is punished with death. The nobleman Claudio is to be executed for sleeping with his betrothed, and his sister, the nun Isabella, supplicates Angelo for his life. Lust for Isabella awakens in Angelo's heart, and he tells her he will free Claudio if she sleeps with him. The Duke, who has remained in Vienna disguised as a monk, arranges to deceive Angelo by sending Mariana, Angelo's former betrothed, whom he cruelly rejected on account of her dowry, to sleep with him in Isabella's stead. Angelo, despite having, as he thinks, slept with Isabella, does not release Claudio, but the gaoler, again prompted by the disguised Duke, sends a different man's head to Angelo, pretending it is Claudio's. The Duke reveals himself, Angelo's perfidy is made public, and yet Mariana pleads for clemency. Isabella joins her, and Angelo is set free.

> LUCIO: The Duke is very strangely gone from
> hence;
> ... Upon his place,
> And with full line of his authority,
> Governs Lord Angelo, a man whose blood
> Is very snow-broth; one who never feels
> The wanton stings and motions of the sense,
> But doth rebate and blunt his natural edge
> With profits of the mind: study and fast.[1]

In *Measure for Measure*, from which these words are taken, the Duke of Vienna wants to reassert law and order to a society that his laid-back rule has brought to licentiousness, but he shrinks from the task himself, aware as he is of his very human, very natural failings.

He is, as Escalus puts it, 'One that, above all other strifes, contended especially to know himself.'[2]

Not only is he aware of his own faults, but he is also wary of what high office is doing to him:

THE DUKE: I love the people,
    But do not like to stage me to their eyes:
    Though it do well, I do not relish well
    Their loud applause, and *aves* [adulation]
      vehement.[3]

The Duke knows himself. But he does not trust himself. Indeed, his lack of self-trust *arises* from his self-knowledge. So, he decides to withdraw from office and put Lord Angelo in his place: 'And with full line of his authority governs Lord Angelo.'[4]

Angelo, 'whose blood is very snow-broth', suffers none of the Duke's qualms about leadership. He has lived an exemplary life, having preferred study and fasting to the sensual pleasures aroused by the society of others. On the face of it, he is a man of tremendous virtue, and he is entirely confident in administering the law that enforces virtue, in letter and spirit.

He is very different from the Duke, who is only too aware of his own fallibility as a human. Angelo trusts himself, but he does not know himself:

ISABELLA: Dressed in a little brief authority,
　Most ignorant of what he's most assured;[5]

This is a conundrum worthy of our exploration, relevant to public life and service. The self-trust that comes from a lack of self-knowledge is a brittle trust indeed and does not make for good leadership. But with self-knowledge often comes a failure of self-trust, a natural modesty and diffidence about leading others, about speaking with confidence, about making decisions. Surely in good leadership both self-knowledge and self-trust are needed, but on the face of it they appear to be incompatible. And so, this essay will explore the conundrum, using *Measure for Measure* as a guide.

Through the character of Angelo, I will explore how disastrous leadership is when it comes from self-trust that depends upon a lack of self-knowledge. Then, through the character of the Duke, I will explore why it is that self-knowledge makes self-trust so hard. And finally, through the character of Isabella, I shall see how these incompatibilities can be resolved. And in the resolution we may find the means to become that rare and valuable thing, a public servant who has both self-trust and self-knowledge.

Self-trust Without Self-knowledge

The Duke is gone, and Angelo sits firmly in his place as ruler of Vienna. He commences his task of dusting off Vienna's long-unenforced laws on sexual behaviour. He orders the closing of the brothels and the sentencing of extramarital fornicators to death. Straight away his 'ignoran[ce] of what he's most assured' is showing itself. His snow-broth blood blinds him to human nature and the laws of supply and demand; he does not see that to succeed in enforcing the laws on sex he will have to 'geld and splay all the youth of the city', as fool and truth-teller Pompey Bum points out: 'If your Worship will take order for the drabs and the knaves, you need not to fear the bawds.'[6]

Pompey the fool has more self-knowledge, and therefore knowledge of human nature, than Angelo. But Angelo is clear and decisive. He does not need to be taught; he believes he has arrived in the post fully morally formed. He has the confidence of one who does not know what he does not know.

A prominent citizen, Claudio, is condemned for sleeping with his betrothed, Juliet, and making her pregnant. They are not married, and this makes Claudio a fornicator in the eyes of the now-active Viennese law, and so his life is forfeit. Angelo condemns him to death. Then Claudio's sister, Isabella, comes to Angelo to plead clemency. But Angelo is firm, stating that if he were in Claudio's place, he would exercise the same judgment on himself. The law is the law, and fornicators must die.

Angelo trusts himself. His certainly allows for no compassion and exercises no restraint on the power he has been given. He is a tyrant, enforcing stability through *external* laws and not by consent – as tyrants have always done, and as they continue to do today. The chastity and good behaviour of the people are the result of a merciless law that makes them so, rather than their own, inner temperance.

Just as the people of Vienna become virtuous only because of an external force, so Angelo's virtue is external only, and as such it does not last. Isabella destroys his carapace of piety. She is a postulant nun from the Order of St Clare, known for its strict rules and discipline, and Angelo, unmoved by bawdy sensuality, is roused to distraction by Isabella's virtue. He has no prior knowledge of hot-blooded lust, born from human fallibility; he does not recognise it or understand it, he only knows what he is feeling. And what is happening inside him is in direct conflict with his outward persona. His trust in himself – or at least, his outward self – is betrayed, deceived. But he is still a leader and he still possesses power, even if it is a power bestowed and not earned, a power born of self-trust and not self-knowledge. This power is incapable of being turned inwards to control his own feelings, which in any case he does not understand, and it lashes outwards to Isabella. To vile purpose.

He tells Isabella, *you can win your brother's pardon, but only by giving your body to me.* He not only tyrannises others but is tyrannised himself, by the hitherto unacknowledged demon within him. Enslaved by it, Angelo is ready to destroy Isabella's chastity – that is to say, her identity, her integrity, her true self. Isabella's chastity has nothing whatsoever in common with Angelo's outward mask of virtue.

THE DUKE: O, what may man within him hide,
　　Though angel on the outward side![7]

And worse still, Angelo does not keep his word and save Claudio's life. After Isabella has – as far as he knows – given in to his demands and lain with him, Angelo repeats his order for Claudio's execution, demanding that the severed head be brought to him as proof that his order has been carried out.

With the help of the Duke, who has disguised himself as a monk, Isabella has in fact arranged things so that, under cover of darkness, Angelo has sex not with her but with his long-abandoned fiancée, Mariana, who inexplicably still loves him. Then, also with the disguised

Duke's help, the prison provost arranges for a substitute head to be brought to Angelo. Isabella remains chaste and Claudio alive. Just as Angelo is deceived in himself, so he is deceived by the world.

That the harm he intended does not come about in no way exonerates Angelo.

Given the right context, our outward confidence is shattered. It is not enough to have self-trust without self-knowledge. My leadership may be powerful, decisive, clear, and undisturbed by doubt, but it will not last because I am human, and I do not escape the fallibility that all humans share. And the failure of my leadership will be all the worse because of the lack of self-knowledge that its strength has depended upon.

Angelo is a character in a play, a drama, but there are real-life examples, such as the highly respected peer who fell spectacularly and sordidly from grace because of a film made public, supposedly shot by the sex workers he was paying. The leak caused outrage because it betrayed a side of him that was the exact opposite of his public self, as a senior member of the House of Lords and upholder of standards. This is an extreme example, but it did not come out of nowhere. People in public office cultivate their exterior selves, the ones on show, to the detriment of their interior selves. In a conversation I recently had with an MP, I suggested that it must be hard to knock on someone's door and ask them to vote for you. 'Not in the least bit hard!' he declared, brazen self-confidence written all over his face. The politician's carapace can be so thick and so well used that you simply cannot see behind it. That person becomes wholly defined by their external persona, and their true inward self is lost. You cannot find them. Can they find themselves?

Politicians *need* self-trust. If we are to continue to elect our leaders – and we must – significant psychological demands will be made on those who stand to be elected. The brazen self-trust that this MP betrayed to me has to be actively cultivated: the willingness and ability to knock on someone's door and ask them to vote for you is just the start. A rhinoceros-hide skin is needed to withstand public and personal abuse online and in real life. One MP told me he was shopping in a supermarket in his constituency when someone came right up to him and said into his face, 'I wouldn't spit on you.' Comments that are made online, to women MPs in particular, and even more so to women MPs of colour, are beyond horrific.

For politicians, there is a need to be decisive in situations when it is impossible to know all the facts; to be able to speak confidently and strongly and with force of opinion every day, locally, nationally, and sometimes internationally; for views to be developed at speed because circumstances are constantly changing – be it those of the pandemic, 'Partygate', Ukraine, the cost-of-living crisis, strikes, or the economy. And those are just the areas of political concern that the public can see.

The confident persona is necessary. The politician is on show, always in the pitiless glare of the public, always transmitting. But the fallible individual, as vulnerable as the rest of us, still lurks behind the carapace, and if that internal self is repressed and concealed, it will emerge disastrously, explosively, into the public sphere, as happened with Angelo – and that unfortunate peer.

Weak interiors need external buttresses to keep them upright. Angelo's weakness is initially concealed by the buttress of the law – external rules that govern behaviour – but when his hot-blooded human interior rebels, he and the law crumble to dust.

The politician's inward self must be attended to. It needs time and a safe space to show its messy workings, its complex desires, both good and bad, so that discernment and integrity have a chance. If politicians are too obsessed with maintaining a squeaky-clean persona, they will inevitably trip up. No one is asking them to do this work, and I worry at how much we focus on external codes and laws to govern – or buttress – the behaviour of our public servants. Better surely to give public figures the space to tend to their inward selves. But it is not easy.

More than that, it is risky. It threatens outward equanimity, undermining the self-trust we need to be leaders. Looking inwards can undo all the superficial self-trust that politicians need just to keep going. It is what leads the Duke to withdraw from public office. So, let us now turn to this conundrum: why is it that self-knowledge makes self-trust so hard to attain?

Self-knowledge Without Self-trust

With the following words the Duke brings Angelo out of his lonely, private life of virtue to take public office:

> Heaven doth with us as we with torches do,
> Not light them for themselves.[8]

These words are deeply ironic. They recall the saying of Jesus. 'No one lighting a lamp puts it in a cellar or under a bushel, but on a stand, that those who enter may see the light' (Luke 11.33). Angelo's 'light' is exterior only, while the Duke's light is born of deep self-knowledge. And yet the Duke plans to hide his own light under a bushel, leaving a tyrant in charge. Why does he do this?

The reason is because it's safer. Hiding my light under a bushel means I do not have to pass judgement. If I am intensely aware of my own failings, how can I stand as a judge of others? How can I cast any stone, let alone the first one? Hiding my light under a bushel means I don't have to express opinions. Do we not find that the more we know on a subject, the less we are willing to comment? The more we understand, the less we criticise and judge?

Hiding my light under a bushel makes me see more clearly, in more nuanced detail. I am backstage, not involved, not taking sides, so I can be impartial, I do not have to have an agenda, I need no angled lens through which to interpret events. It is no accident that civil servants temperamentally shrink from the limelight. Their task is to understand thoroughly the policy area on which they then give advice to politicians, privately, and not in the full glare of publicity. They may well have wise things to say about the world, born of their study, but we will not hear them share these insights publicly. If your temperament is to speak loudly and publicly, you should not be a civil servant. But if you speak in public, even if you know what you are talking about, not all the subtleties of the subject are going to be able to be expressed, let alone heard. Nuance is usually forfeit when it is brought into the light.

Hiding my light under a bushel protects my integrity because it is not threatened by the effect that others might have on me. Bringing my light out into the world makes it vulnerable to the world. The Duke believes that in order to enforce the law he will have to become someone he is not; he will have to develop intolerance, to become confrontational:

> Sith 'twas my fault to give the people scope,
> 'Twould be my tyranny to strike and gall them
> For what I bid them do.[9]

He believes that his soft, self-aware, fallible interiority will have to harden if he is to rule as he thinks he should.

Hiding my light under a bushel protects me from arrogance and conceit. The Duke knows that he is susceptible – we all are – to the people's *aves*. Celebrity status, the myth of greatness, that particular temptation of politicians to have their fragile, well-intentioned egos recognised and applauded. The results of this hubris are often dangerous and short-lived.

Hiding my light under a bushel protects others from being harmed by me. If I act, especially if I have power, I always run the risk of bringing more harm than good to the world. Take unconscious biases: I know I have them. But by their nature, I don't know what they are. I only know that since I have them, my speech may unintentionally disparage cultures and perspectives other than my own. And the trouble is, it is only as my words are spoken that my unconscious bias becomes conscious to me, and by then it is too late. The prejudice is spoken, the offence is committed, the harm is done. Better to remain silent. Better to hide my light under a bushel – not least because there will often be an Angelo-style response to our failings, an impetus to condemn without mercy a sin that is in all of us.

And so, with my light hidden cravenly under a bushel, my talent safely buried, I am paralysed. The lack of self-trust from an increase in self-knowledge brings about an inability to act, a wish to withdraw from public life – a wish not to be required to lead, as the Duke found.

Yuval Levin, commenting on trends in the US, calls this paralysis 'distorted passivity', a growing phenomenon caused by excessive risk aversion:

> [We have] a rising generation acutely averse to risk, and so to every form of dynamism. Excessive risk aversion now often deforms parenting, education, work, leadership, and fellowship in our society. It is intertwined with a more general tendency toward inhibition and constriction – with Americans walking on eggshells around each other in many of our major institutions, and with codes of speech and conduct becoming increasingly prevalent.[10]

Needless to say, the online world facilitates this trend, allowing more and more people to live, in Levin's words, 'as functional loners, meeting their needs with a minimum of eye contact or interpersonal risk'.

A distorted passivity, a riskless loneliness, has us curled up in front of a screen in our bedrooms, avoiding eye contact. But – another irony – there are no bushels in the online world to hide under; rather there is total exposure. Online I can be seen by the indiscriminate masses, and far more of me can be seen than most of us realise, as we unwittingly expose our preferences to algorithms – algorithms that nudge us into extreme positions and the joys and perils of personalised advertising.

So, are we to be stuck with this? If self-trust comes only from a lack of self-knowledge, then are those confident enough to lead, to speak, to act, by the very same token exterior beings, all surface and no substance, unwise and unaware?

God help us all if that be so.

Self-trust Arising From the Journey to Self-knowledge

In the final scene of *Measure for Measure*, the Duke has resumed his seat of authority. He decrees that Angelo's life is forfeit for his truly horrible deeds. At this point,

Isabella and Mariana still believe that Claudio is dead by Angelo's hand, and yet they plead for Angelo's life. In so doing, they begin to show us *how* self-knowledge can serve good leadership. Mariana argues:

> They say
> Best men are moulded out of faults;
> And, for the most, become much more the better
> For being a little bad.[12]

This is a tender, economic elucidation of the role of penitence in public service. Yes, I am not good, but I am aware that I am not good, and I am penitent. A public servant can never be wholly good, but if they are penitent, they may be worthy of our mercy. This makes them porous rather than impermeable, as their carapace of false virtue is pierced and light shines on their vulnerable, fallible self, which has its part to play. Angelo's fall from grace and subsequent remorse aligns him more closely to the Duke. It makes him attend to his interior, and so has the potential to make him a better leader.

And Isabella, who is in the deepest pain at the loss of her brother by the hand of this man, the same man who sought to destroy her integrity and self-esteem by violating her chastity, is prevailed upon by Mariana to join her in pleading for Angelo's life. Angelo's! After being asked three times to help, Isabella kneels in solidarity with Mariana, perhaps recalling her own earlier words:

> Why all the souls that were were forfeit once,
> And He that might the vantage best have took
> Found out the remedy.[13]

And here we have the bringing together of wisdom with action, of self-knowledge with self-trust. It is Christ of whom Isabella speaks, who has the best vantage of our faults, who sees all but neither administers the letter of the law in judgement of us, nor simply sits and watches as we mess up our lives. He 'found out the remedy'.

What is 'the remedy'? Isabella herself lives it out when she finds the will to plea for mercy for Angelo, *even whilst in the throes of the pain he has caused her*. Remember, at this point she still believes her brother is dead by Angelo's hand.

So, this is what I would say to the conundrum of self-knowledge and self-trust. I would say that we must walk towards our inward selves and acknowledge what is there, however painful. I would say that the tremulous yet determined and courageous facing of our fallibility will bring us strength to lead – real strength; real inner confidence; real inner self-trust.

By this means, those in public office, the powerful, are

brought to self-restraint without surrendering responsibility; they are kept porous without losing a sense of self. This is such important work for our public servants to undertake. It isn't easy, and there isn't much help on offer. Westminster Abbey Institute is trying to address this, working especially with younger public servants. Inspired by the case of the respected peer whose interior lusts were filmed for all to see, we have created a residential programme called 'Facing Fallibility through Tragedy and Comedy'. In the first part of the programme, we learn an Ignatian technique of quietly, silently feeling our way into ourselves, to the place where we are most vulnerable, most ashamed, the place or rather person whom we would rather others never saw. And we sit there, making friends with our shadow selves. We are not trying to solve anything. We just sit, as you might with a beloved who is in great pain, and whose pain you cannot take away, but whom you are not going to desert either. And gradually, as you become more and more at ease with this deepest fear, something creative happens. Joy emerges. You have faced the worst in yourself, and you find not desolation but deep joy and deep strength, right inside yourself. That is how we spend the morning: in quiet, gentle, vulnerable meditation.

And then, after lunch, we have a stand-up comedy workshop. We play games to make friends with our inner fool, the one whose voice we dare not speak out loud, especially as public servants – our unedited voice. And we discover it is, like Shakespeare's fool, both very funny and truthful. In *Measure for Measure*, Pompey Bum sees far more than Angelo ever can.

The Facing Fallibility residential is not for the faint-hearted, but work like this is essential for those in positions of public service. We must take care of our inner selves. Never has it felt more important to do everything we can to strengthen leadership by consent, through the arts of self-knowledge, tolerance, listening to others, and finding trust and truth in ourselves.

I am grateful for the observations of Declan Donnellan, G. Wilson Knight, Robert W. Chambers, Aleks Krotoski, Yuval Levin, Seán Moore, and above all William Shakespeare, which contributed to this essay.

Trust in Oneself: A Response

Josie Rourke

Any appeal to temper power with an understanding of what makes us all human, which Claire's essay has done, feels essential at the moment. We should all derive great comfort from her hopeful progress with the Westminster Abbey Institute towards a more compassionate and honest public life.

I know *Measure for Measure* horribly well, and it was wonderful to be returned to it through the prism of Claire's lecture and essay. It was my set text for A Levels, and when I showed up at university to study English, I was told that I'd be spending another two years with the play. It's also the most recent Shakespeare play I have directed. So, either I've trailed about after the play or *Measure for Measure* has been in pursuit of me for over twenty years.

Measure for Measure is what's known in the trade as a 'Shakespearean problem play'. This is a category distinct from his other plays that fall into histories, comedies, tragedies, romances, and the Roman plays. If I tell you that *Measure for Measure* sits in a group with Shakespeare's *Troilus and Cressida* and his *All's Well That Ends Well*, you might recognise – perhaps just by virtue of not recognising those titles – that they are amongst the less frequently staged of The Complete Works. It is not because they're bad; it's because they're tough. Well, they're problem plays. Problem plays are resoundingly uncommercial. They don't satisfy or pay off, and their set-piece scenes are often confounding. They generally unsettle the audience and can leave a bad taste in their mouths.

As Claire conveys in the essay preceding this one, Shakespeare's problem plays often do not trust themselves. They can certainly retreat from our understanding. And I can report from experience that, for a director in rehearsal, at the point of their most difficult twists these plays can appear also not to know themselves. Not a day goes by while directing *Measure for Measure* that an actor doesn't ask, 'Why does he/she do that?' I often do not know the answer.

There is – sometimes – an incorrect presumption that playwrights sit down with the plot all planned out before writing a word, as opposed to just setting a handful of characters off on a series of scenes and waiting to see what happens. Though I don't know it to be true,

I once heard a story that a famous actor, while playing Rosalind in *As You Like It*, was heard to shout in rehearsals, 'My character wouldn't say that!' It's pretty tough to get a rewrite on a 400-year-old play, but I sympathise.

I once studied with a playwright and director who told me that, if there had been literary managers or dramaturges in Shakespeare's day, he would still be at his desk rewriting the fourth act of *Measure for Measure* for them. Certainly, these problem plays do not reassure or console the watcher with a neat conclusion. That kind of straightforward catharsis only comes from the multiple deaths of the tragedies or the many marriages of the comedies.

The other problem with problem plays is that you're never really told what you're meant to think of the characters' actions. Perhaps because of Angelo's and the Duke's behaviour, the state of Vienna in *Measure for Measure* does not feel purged or healed of impurities by the end of the play. In Act V, Isabella calls for justice by shouting the word five times at a public meeting. And yet the citizens at the meeting accuse her of being mad, and the play leaves us with an uncertain pardon, a possible execution, an unhappy marriage, and an unanswered proposal. No real justice there. Compare this with *Hamlet*'s neat nine deaths and final words, 'the rest is silence'.

As an artistic director, when considering whether to

take on a new play I always ask myself, how likely is it to spark healthy debate? Will people be talking about it on the bus home? This was a frequent test question in our weekly programming meetings. In the case of *Measure for Measure*, members of the audience, after seeing the play, might debate whether Isabella does the right thing in refusing to sleep with Angelo and save her brother's life. Or they might dispute if the Duke is guilty of setting up Angelo for an inevitable fall. Is it a selfish power play or a prudent sacrifice for the good of the state on his part? The play does not answer these questions, and with its wilfully uneven conclusion, *Measure for Measure* rates high in its potential to sow debate, and perhaps even discord, among viewers on the bus home. But despite this potential, these wonderfully knotty problem plays are not popular plays. They don't satisfy the viewers' bloodlust like tragedy or provide the sugar rush of comedy.

In another part of my life, I direct films for commercial entities such as American studios. The majority of script notes I receive from executives focus on whether conclusions are 'satisfying' or characters are 'delivering'. Is that character 'likeable'? Are they 'relatable'? Does their story 'pay off'? Are we meant to like this character or not like them? The clearest example of this in my career was in the development of the script for a film I directed, *Mary*

Queen of Scots, which prompted endless debates with executives and editors as to whether or not the titular Mary should be 'likeable' – not a term I suspect Mary Queen of Scots ever troubled to apply to herself. This search for certainty in character and story is a little like the formulation of the self-certain leader, Angelo, which Claire unpacked for us in her essay. It hints at a collective impulse towards perfectionism: our tendency as viewers to prize smoothness above grittiness, completeness above uncertainty. Nothing should be so uneven as to upset us too much. The following scenes will not be disturbing. Please keep your hands inside the car for the duration of the ride. As these film-direction notes often come from LA, I sometimes wonder if this search for certainty might be related to California's expectation of 278 days of sunshine each year. This is comparable to the friction-less satisfaction of being served personalised advertising by an algorithm, which Claire identifies in her essay. Your phone, your weather, your shopping experience – everything is offered with a pleasingly rounded edge.

Like many of us in the pandemic years, I've cherished laughter wherever I can find it. Mid-pandemic, people started joking that they were 'not enjoying Season 2 of Covid'. We have become so used to stories being satisfying that the pandemic itself began to resemble a television show with no narrative arc. A 'bad season' of Covid;

it was boring us. Something enjoyable must have a beginning, a middle, and an end, and we must be allowed to complete it. But we are confusing narrative neatness with meaning. We think meaning is neatness, certainty. To viewers, meaning is conclusion; it is pay-off. If meaning were a character, it would be, to apply Claire's idea of the self-certain leader, Angelo. It is confident. Confident enough to knock on your door and ask for your vote.

In these problem plays, credits do not reassuringly roll over a story well resolved. Although Isabella's plea for clemency for Angelo, the abuser who she believes has killed her brother, is exceptionally moving and wholly commendable, overall her virtue does not triumph and the state is not cleansed of corruption. In fact, there is a notorious and horrifying final moment in which the Duke, who has been secretly surveilling everyone and assisting Isabella while disguised as a monk, unmasks and asks her to marry him. Perhaps unsurprisingly, she does not utter a further word in the drama, either of acceptance or refusal, frustration or despair. Academics write very powerfully about how much a fine actress might do with that silence. I am here to tell you that the fine actress would absolutely prefer to have some lines.

As Claire wonderfully points out in her essay, these problem plays create discomfort and unearth neuroticism through their characters' quest for self-knowledge.

In the tragedy *Oedipus*, the titular character hurtles like a high-speed train towards his tragic fate, as prophesied by the Delphic oracle, and the audience is granted catharsis when the truth is revealed; Oedipus finally 'know[s] thyself', and the city of Thebes is cleansed by his ultimate self-sacrifice. By contrast, the protagonists of *Measure for Measure* are left completely at sea, unknown to themselves, and the city of Vienna is quite likely to be destroyed as a result. At the beginning of the play the Duke leaves Angelo in charge and then, within a handful of scenes, he has dressed up as a monk and is meddling in Angelo's horrible wrongdoings. The Duke is an incompetent voyeur. He is isolated but still interfering in events, his monk's robes putting him at a safe remove from his subjects. By the time we get to Act IV, even the Duke has lost the thread of his plans. Neither he nor Angelo can be trusted and, as Claire so astutely identifies, there seems to be a dissonance between their exterior life and their interior world that starts to threaten all around them.

Where I diverge slightly from Claire in my interpretation of the play is that I don't really believe the Duke: I think he talks a good game. But then again, I don't trust anyone who borrows a habit and passes himself off as a monk. Indeed, there's quite a lot of scholarship that believes this character is Shakespeare's take on Machiavelli's *Prince*, but that's for another lecture.

Angelo's outer certainty, of which Claire writes, doesn't just falter but evaporates on meeting Isabella. It's gone in fewer than 160 lines. These are all the lines it takes for Angelo to turn to the audience and ask them to identify a weird sensation – in Claire's helpful formulation, the shattering of 'outward confidence'. 'What's this? What's this?' Angelo asks. This novel sensation Angelo experiences is far from wholesome. Indeed, it is not only his lust for Isabella he feels rising within him, but also a growing sense of the power he might hold over her in the pursuit of that lust. Heady. Creepy. Very wrong.

Hamlet hesitates and dies; Lear is mad and dies; Othello is jealous and dies; Macbeth is ambitious and dies; Romeo is in love and... you get the picture. Angelo and the Duke live and are... what? Who knows? Can they be trusted? They are extremely adept at announcing one intention and then pursuing an entirely different one. Up until the moment the Duke produces his weird bed-swap solution, Isabella has refused to yield to Angelo's indecent proposal and seems prepared to let her brother die to preserve her chastity and with it her immortal soul. None of these characters would make it past a modern-day studio executive. I can hear them asking, 'Can we do something to make them more likeable?'

To direct actors in these roles is to turn up every day and rehearse a twisting, inconsistent series of actions.

The struggle is whether to confer coherence on the story or embrace the chaos. The arrogant, confident part of me – perhaps the one whom people most readily recognise as the character of a theatre director – wants to swish about brandishing an interpretation. It wants to tell the actor, the audience member, the critic what to think of the play and how to judge these characters. That is – more often than not – the route to a critically successful production. An even easier route to critical success is to avoid these problem plays altogether.

And yet I push aside the comedies and tragedies and turn myself towards these problem plays. It might be that the process of directing a problem play reveals to me more of my flawed and contradictory self than the directing of a *Hamlet* or a *King Lear*. To choose to direct a problem play, I must acknowledge its flaws and embrace the possibility that I might fail with critics or even on my own terms. Perhaps by facing the inherent difficulties of the play, by encountering likely failure, I might arrive at a more honest account of my own life and self. Because – as Claire puts it much more eloquently – it is our responsibility to face the troubling and difficult things, within our problem selves, within these problem plays. And to move forward in the hope of a more compassionate life, self, and – perhaps – story.

Trust in Institutions

Anthony Ball

In 2021 Bill Gates, a renowned optimist, expressed the fear that in 2022 'decreased trust in institutions might be the biggest obstacle standing in our way'. Twenty years previously, the chairman of Unilever, Niall FitzGerald, said in an address to the Advertising Association: 'Whether we're selling a political message or a packet of cereal, everyone in the communications business is now faced with a fundamental decline in trust.'

So, one of the things we ought to do is check the facts. Is it true that trust in institutions has diminished? And, if so, how far? A slight spoiler alert – the answer is 'yes, it has', but it is interesting to dig into that generalisation. It is also worth asking the question, as a recent UN report on trust in public institutions began by doing: 'Why should we care about trust?'[1] Indeed, what do we really mean by 'trust' in this context, given the range of ways the word or concept is used? Is the one who is expected to do the trusting significant? That is a fair amount of ground to cover within the confines of this essay, and I will attempt to do so, additionally honouring Westminster Abbey Institute's aim to revitalise moral and spiritual values in public life by offering some practical suggestions on what might be done about all this.

Definitions

Trust is a multidimensional and multi-layered phenomenon.[2] Concepts of trust, trustworthiness, integrity, confidence, competency, and expertise, for instance, may all be rolled into one single-issue question about trust in surveys and opinion polls. How these concepts and the term 'trust' are actually interpreted will vary across countries and cultures, but a simple and intuitive understanding will suffice for our purposes. In its research, the Organisation for Economic Co-operation and Development (OECD) defines trust as 'a person's belief that another person or institution will act consistently with their expectations of positive behaviour'.[3] Although that is indeed sufficient for our purposes, it reveals the distinction that literature on trust typically makes between horizontal trust (the trust members of a community have in each other) and vertical trust (the trust members of a community have in the institutions of that community).

Doubt might now arise as to whether the title 'Trust in Institutions' means that this essay will explore trust *within* public service institutions (the horizontal) or whether it will be looking at trust *of* these institutions by citizens (the vertical). My focus will be on the latter, although the reader does need to keep in mind the former. The question of whether and why public servants within an institution are trusted is an integral component of how that institution as a whole is regarded. To achieve trust, an institution has to be trustworthy, and this depends, crucially, on how its officials perform and how their acts are experienced by citizens.

Taking an overview of some recent findings, we might note that the trust considered here is often called 'reflective' or 'contingent' trust. There are other kinds of trust, like 'innocent' (as held by young children) or 'implicit' (as found in committed personal relationships), but they are not so relevant to this essay. We should, however, recognise that the generation of trust is the result of different processes. A cognitive process is rational and based on what happens in the real world (even if mediated by subjective factors). An affective process, by contrast, is based on what an individual has been raised to believe and can be mixed with stereotyping (positive or negative) based on different forms of identity. The relative weight of cognitive and affective drivers of trust is likely to vary significantly across contexts,[4] but it is important to factor this distinction into our thinking, as it is relevant to how different sections of society respond in giving or withholding trust – and, as society is diverse, it serves as a reminder to expect such differences.

Evidence for Current Levels of Trust in Institutions

The polls and research into the question of trust in government and public institutions are fairly extensive, both in the UK and internationally. Much of the learning that might be achieved from them can come from attending to detail and acknowledging the need for nuance. For example, if looking at the generally very high degree of trust in the police force or the legal system in the UK, which consistently outstrips trust in government, it is easy to be complacent and feel the focus for improvement should be elsewhere. That is, until we break down the groups that have delivered the overall response and find that trust is much lower amongst ethnic minorities. Or, as the Victims Commissioner reported from a survey published in September 2021, just 43 per cent of victims would report a crime to the police again, and the percentage of victims that would attend court again was down to 50 per cent from 67 per cent the previous year.

The trend regarding trust in politicians is unlikely to surprise: in 1944, one in three British people (35 per cent) saw politicians as merely 'out for themselves', while by 2014 that number had grown to 48 per cent. New polling by the Institute for Public Policy Research, published in December 2021, had 63 per cent stating that they share this view – nearly two in three people.[5]

Little wonder, then, that the Edelman Trust Barometer declared in January 2022: 'We find a world ensnared in a vicious cycle of distrust, fuelled by a growing lack of faith in media and government. Through disinformation and division, these two institutions are feeding the cycle and exploiting it for commercial and political gain.'[6] The May 2020 Edelman Trust Barometer reported a surge of trust in government, 'when the world sought leadership capable of tackling a global pandemic';[7] this proved to be a trust bubble, after a stuttering response saw trust in government in the UK fall back to 42 per cent in 2021 (although trust in UK health authorities rose to 74 per cent). On the media side, fear of fake news is running at an all-time high of 76 per cent globally (although 'only' 65 per cent in the UK).[8]

It can be instructive to draw on the international context. A United Nations report last year on trust in public institutions identified that:

Data from opinion surveys across a broad[er] range of countries show a decline in trust in most public bodies since 2000. The percentage of people expressing confidence or trust in their Governments in the 62 developed and developing countries included peaked at 46 per cent on average in 2006, and fell to 36 per cent by 2019.[9]

By looking at this at the macro level the UN also noted that 'Higher income countries tend to enjoy higher levels of institutional trust than lower income countries ... while opinion polls also suggest that trust in national Government is higher in countries with authoritarian Governments than in those with established democracies.'[10]

Why Trust in Institutions Matters

That last finding is somewhat problematic for those who think, as the OECD does, that:

Trust is the foundation for the legitimacy of public institutions and a functioning democratic system. It is crucial for maintaining political participation and social cohesion ... Trust is important for the success of a wide range of public policies that depend on behavioural responses from the public. For example, public trust leads to greater compliance with regulations and the tax system. In the longer term, trust is needed to tackle long-term societal challenges such as climate change, ageing populations, and the automation of work.[11]

In general terms, we can say that 'trust in each other, in our public institutions and in our leaders are all essential ingredients for social and economic progress, allowing people to cooperate with and express solidarity for one another'.[12] Its absence is seen as contributing to, *inter alia*, support for extreme political views, increasing public discontent, and protests that have resulted in violent conflict. On one occasion when he spoke to the Security Council, in 2020, the UN secretary-general warned of a 'trust deficit' that threatens to undermine progress towards the internationally agreed Sustainable Development Goals.[13]

Yet the issue does bite closer to home too. The creation and rapid deployment of vaccines against Covid-19 was a truly remarkable achievement, so the refusal of so many people around the world to get vaccinated was and remains a real problem, and a stark indicator of the severity of what can be described as a current crisis in public trust.

What Can be Done About the Failure of Trust in Institutions?

Niall FitzGerald, quoted in the opening paragraph of this essay, went on to say:

You can have all the facts and figures, all the supporting evidence, all the endorsement that you want, but if you don't command trust, you won't get anywhere. And trust, of course, is the one thing that can't be built in a one-off spate of advertising. Trust is built over the long term, on the basis not of communication but of action. And then again, trust, once established, can be lost in an instant – one ill-judged remark and it's gone forever.

If 'gone forever' is true, it renders otiose the question of what public servants and citizens might be able to do about this decline in trust. Thankfully, it is an exaggeration, and it *is* possible to rebuild trust. It just takes time and patience, energy, and effort. Trust will grow as people experience trustworthy behaviour; when they see actions consistent with words, and the words are ones they understand and relate to; when they feel respected and understood. That places a premium on response and communication, at both an institutional and individual-public-servant level on the one hand, and at an individual and community level on the other.

It should be obvious that a 'one size fits all' approach is not going to make much headway. With different individuals and communities starting in very different places, the response to any given initiative is going to differ. If trust is to be built based on outcomes as they are actually experienced, then there has to be an investment in working out how to achieve those outcomes. It is more complex than being able to claim 'fairness' or 'justice' (and so trustworthiness) by pointing to equality of inputs if the outcomes continue to deliver or even exacerbate inequalities.

In turning to some practical ways in which this trust-rebuilding operation might be undertaken by public institutions and those serving within them, it is perhaps reassuring to find that the literature emerging from the significant amount of research undertaken on the issue, some of which has already been referenced, converges around very similar drivers or themes. I will briefly review some of these, recognising that they will not all matter equally in different circumstances, before concluding with a personal formulation.

OECD work has identified five main public governance drivers of trust in government institutions: responsiveness, reliability, integrity, fairness, and openness. A slightly dated MORI report from 2002 noted that 'the public' were demanding information and openness, independence, and more personable services as conditions for developing trust. Interestingly the UN has reservations about openness or transparency, noting (but, to be fair, not advancing) the argument that 'in some cases increased transparency may hinder trust by opening public institutions to just and unjust blame equally and by creating unsustainable pressure on already overstretched public administrations'.[14] The UN flags effectiveness, fairness, and responsiveness as the key components to building trust.[15] In a recent paper, the consultancy company Deloitte boiled the necessary components down to competence and intent,[16] which is mirrored by what Margaret Levi pointed out nearly twenty-five years previously: 'The major sources of distrust in government are promise-breaking, incompetence, and the antagonism of government actors toward those they are supposed to serve.'[17] Matthew Bishop, writing earlier this year for the Edelman Trust Institute, also saw what has created the crisis in trust as hypocrisy, incompetence, over-promising, and the infodemic.[18]

This last point, that trust has suffered due to a rise in misinformation and disinformation, is in one way or another acknowledged by most current commentators. It takes us back to the other quotation in the opening paragraph, from Bill Gates. He pins much of the blame for decreased trust in institutions on growing polarisation, in which social media 'has played a huge role in spreading misinformation that makes people suspicious about their governments'. And it is not just governments that are being hit by this so-called infodemic. Gates himself was at the centre of one wild conspiracy theory popular among anti-vaxxers – that he would use the vaccination programme to microchip humanity – as they received and spread misinformation about medical science.

As Claire Gilbert touched upon in her essay, the ability of social media to target or match information and recipients in a self-referential bubble is problematic. But it also shows that it should be possible to exploit the technology to tailor institutional communication with and to groups where lack of trust is an issue.

Values for Rebuilding Trust: A Personal Formulation

The four characteristics I believe should be advanced in order to improve the public's trust in institutions are: honesty, humility, compassion, and competence. If these are to be characteristics of the institutions themselves then they also need to be features of the behaviour of the public servants within the institutions. If the public servants act in these ways, they will contribute to building a trusting environment *within* the institutions as well as enhancing the public's trust of the institutions. I do not pretend that these four characteristics equal a comprehensive list or recipe for solving the crisis in trust, but they do – in my view– represent essential components in reversing the decline in trust. Each could merit an essay of their own! They are intertwined and, whilst they can apply to everyone, Christians would certainly be able to recognise them as spiritual values that connect with their faith. Whilst they can be subjected to the requirement to be codified and measured for outcome and impact, as values they are likely to be more effective when applied to that elusive goal of culture change. As Gilbert observes, a focus on codes and standards, legislating for what must be done, could well prove less effective than investing in an internal transformation of character.

Perhaps it is worth saying that, because of the observation made earlier about why trust matters, this essay assumes that an increase in trust in public institutions and public servants is desirable. It is not argued here that trust is necessary to deliver on objectives, although I *do* believe that to be true, at least over the long term. In the short term it is certainly possible to be dishonest and get elected, be incompetent or arrogant and receive public funds, indifferent or unaccountable, and still have people use your services.

Honesty

Honesty applies internally (personally and institutionally) and externally (in terms of what is communicated). The former links closely to the self-knowledge theme addressed earlier by Gilbert. Institutions as well as individuals need to understand themselves and know their strengths and weaknesses. In addition to ensuring that they are not deluded about their own successes and failures, this will help them to be realistic about what it is possible to achieve, on which there is further comment below, under 'humility'.

Honesty with and towards external stakeholders is also important, as is making sure that what you say and what you do are aligned. In an individual's personal life, it is a well-known experience that trust in a third party is undermined if it is discovered they have lied to that individual. Hypocrisy destroys trust. Institutions also need to be honest about the motivations behind policies so that people know that things are done in their best interests.

Ensuring that 'people know', in other words good communication, is a crucial element of the 'honesty' value. The discussion earlier about the infodemic highlights the need for institutions to be seen as reliable sources of information and to be proactive in ensuring that information is disseminated. Fake news can go viral very quickly, so a rapid response in combatting it is essential. Many public institutions have a powerful communications machinery at their disposal and need to demonstrate trustworthiness in how it is used if it is to retain effectiveness.

A policy of 'intelligent openness' should be pursued that allows:

> Information to be accessible, understandable, useable, and assessable. This means, in practice, making all data and information used in decision making to be seen and understood clearly and easily by the public [and] to ensure that it is possible for anyone interested to check the sources and quality of the evidence, and the integrity of the decision-making process.[19]

There should be no hiding of unpleasant truths in unintelligible jargon or phrasing things in a way that tries to lead people to a conclusion rather than allowing them to judge for themselves.

Of course, institutions – governments or political parties, for example – need to be able to 'sell' their message and policies, to emphasise the positive in their achievements or minimise those of their opponents. But there is a balance to be struck between an expected and accepted level of 'spin' and misrepresenting the truth in a way that undermines the trustworthiness of the message or the medium. It could be argued, and indeed on occasion it has been, that some of the claims advanced during recent election or referendum campaigns are so unreliable as to undermine the legitimacy of the result.

Lastly under this value, and linked to the next one, humility, is the question of admitting to – rather than trying to cover up or justify – mistakes, whether for the protection of the individual or the institution. We can all think of examples where such behaviour has damaged trust. Like it or not, the clergy must face up to the effect of the safeguarding scandal on public trust in the Church. The Church is learning, too slowly at times and hardly at all in some countries, that an honest admission of what went wrong and a sincere apology (especially to those harmed but also to the public at large) that seeks to put things right and explain what has been or will be done to avoid a recurrence are the means to restoring trust.

Humility

Admitting mistakes requires humility. It requires the hard work of self-examination which, as suggested earlier, will also help develop a realistic picture of what can be achieved. Knowingly over-promising falls foul of the requirement for honesty, and restoring trust may also require a levelling with the public so that, alongside dropping unrealistic claims to have all the answers, there is also a resetting of citizens' expectations of institutions and public servants. As well as fostering more realistic expectations, there should be a desire and willingness for collaboration with others (including with political opponents and across borders) to address the complex problems of our world.

A recognition of the complexity of the issues in question should naturally lead to a recognition of the need for partnership and an acceptance that it is simply improbable, if not impossible, to consistently get all the answers right when tackling such complex challenges. In the Covid pandemic, for example, balancing the competing demands from the public for effective healthcare, economic prosperity, and personal freedoms was bound to lead to controversial choices.

Knowing that mistakes and wrong decisions will sometimes be made should inform an approach to engaging with the public and delivering services that works against arrogance, particularly if combined with a commitment to honesty. Arrogance can lead to a cavalier attitude to risk, which in itself can undermine trust. In general, false alarms are forgiven more readily than missed chances to stop a bad event, possibly because it is a way of assessing motives (does this person/institution prioritise *our* lives/wellbeing over the disruption to *their* agenda?). Although it is true that 'single negative events have a greater impact than positive ones, a positive pattern of behaviour or policy can sometimes outweigh a single negative event'.[20] That should give public servants the confidence to achieve a trust-inducing balance between precaution and risk-taking.

It is also worth making the connection between humility and communication. We have already mentioned the 'transmit' element, but the 'receive' element is just as important. The institution may think it has the answers, but are they answers to the actual questions or needs of the public? Just as communication needs to recognise diverse audiences, so too does listening. An election manifesto, for example, necessarily covers a range of policies and proposals. Acting as if winning an election indicates majority approval for the implementation of all of them has the potential to engender cynicism and distrust towards the system. Indeed, listening to those who feel or are marginalised by the democratic system is going to be necessary if trust in that system, and its institutions, is to be enhanced and the 'participation ladder' climbed.

There is a final point to cover under humility: that of accountability. If power corrupts, then those seeking and exercising it, or the institutions that mediate it, need to be particularly careful to ensure that there are healthy mechanisms of accountability in place. Confidence or trust is needed in them. Humility demands that institutions and public servants are open to being held accountable. Self-regulation – whether in the media, higher education, the judiciary, the police, or, indeed, the Church – have all been questioned in recent years as doubts are raised about the extent to which independent scrutiny is really delivered.

Independent accountability can be compromised in many ways, and trust inevitably suffers as a result. Emaciated funding is one. For example, the budget of the Equality and Human Rights Commission (EHRC) has gone from £70 million at its launch in 2007 to £17 million in 2022, which, as Lord Woolley has pointed out,[21] is less than the Commission for Racial Equality had in its final year (2007) for a narrower remit. With the issues raised by the Black Lives Matter movement still very much to the fore, what message does that – or the current absence of any Black commissioners on the EHRC – send about the government's attentiveness to these sections of our society?

Compassion

That question offers a link to the next value in my list, compassion, or humanity. Discrimination destroys trust, whereas behaviours that demonstrate value and respect for everyone, regardless of background, identity, or belief, will tend to build it up. People want to be treated as individuals and to know that they are being treated fairly. Public institutions should be impartial in performing their functions and be seen to promote a fair distribution of economic resources. As noted under 'humility', institutions and the public servants within them that show – by deed and communication – that their motivations and the policies they generate are for the broader good of society, the wellbeing of the body of citizens as a whole, and not just 'compliance' or 'efficiency', will be more trusted. People respond to compassion – towards themselves and others When the war in Ukraine broke out, for example, a flood of people registered under the scheme to sponsor or take in a Ukrainian refugee; the widespread administrative difficulty in doing so was laid at the door of the government and their apparent focus on fulfilling the requirements of the visa system rather than meeting people's needs.

As government services increasingly move online and call centres replace face-to-face interactions, a move accelerated by the protective measures required by the Covid pandemic, it will be essential not to lose sight of the results of research showing that people tend to trust more those with whom they have most contact, such as front-line staff, while being more suspicious of 'bureaucrats' or 'management'. Research shows that people are also inclined to make a distinction between individuals working for an organisation, especially when encountering them in person, and the organisation as a whole.[22] The former tend to be trusted more.

Competence

Of course, trust is also generated by the experience of having expectations met, of enjoying services, information, or programmes that are delivered reliably, consistently, and in a timely manner. My final value, competence, has a more operational character than the others and it is closely linked to capability. An institution or individual that does not possess the means or the resources to do what is expected of them is unlikely to succeed and – as has been observed throughout – failure will tend to undermine trust.

In an increasingly digital environment, citizens want to be confident that the institutions with which they interact are holding and using their personal data responsibly. Time and again, research shows that responsiveness in delivering public services has the highest influence on trust in government and the civil service locally and nationally.[23] The public, and the individuals who form it, want to know that people are doing their best for them, meeting their needs, and delivering on expectations. Trust increases when that happens.

This connects with the simple and common-sense definition of trust at the start of this essay. In looking at this in relation to public institutions, it could said they are given a mandate by the public and they earn trust by compassionately and competently implementing this mandate. Of course, simplicity is not always the solution, and 'the people' as a conceptual category is ill-suited to capture the complexity of citizenry. Society is obviously not a homogeneous body but rather a multiplicity of identities and interests, often in conflict with each other. As public institutions seek to build trust in such a context, with and through humility and honesty, it is critical that any analysis of how to proceed reflects this diversity and gives adequate attention to the impact of these different social cleavages.

That, in a way, provides a link to James Hawkey's reflections in the following essay. Before turning the page, however, a concluding thought that derives from the proposition in the chapter's title, 'Trust in Institutions': is there much chance of the public having trust in an *institution* (vertical), a government department, say, if those within it don't trust *each other* (horizontal)? If, for example, ministers don't listen to the advice of their civil servants, however well argued, or if civil servants are afraid or no longer feel it worthwhile to give their best impartial advice to their political masters? That is where the vertical and the horizontal aspects of trust come together – somewhat appropriately for Westminster Abbey Institute, forming a cross.

Trust in People

James Hawkey

Is suspicion of others natural or not? To give anything like a complete answer to this extremely complex question, we would first need to establish the grounds of our analysis. We would need to consider themes including nature, sin, creation, community, and intention. In what we call the Judaeo-Christian tradition, mutual suspicion is certainly not what humans are called to, and certainly not what we are made for. The opposite of suspicion is trust. And yet, to trust is to risk, to trust is to make vulnerable, and to trust is to place the centre of our universe somewhere other than ourselves. The Greek word for trust used by the New Testament writers is the same as that used for faith – *pistis*, or its verb form, *pisteuó*; from trust can come faithfulness, reliability, that-which-can-be-believed. So, trust in people needs to be interrogated alongside other forms of trust, faith, or belief. Trust is certainly necessary for the functioning and flourishing of a healthy society, but it is also a choice. Trust can't be injected into the social system like a vaccine or an anti-dote. Conditions must be created to make trust realistic, or even, perhaps, worthwhile. We need cultures of trust in which people can be formed in the family, in school, in the local community. These networks, by which people learn together what trust is, provide a forma-tion in habit that can become a societal pattern. Cyni-cism becomes all too easy when those conditions are frequently absent or routinely undermined. For religious people, *hope* becomes possible in that which is not seen, precisely because of what they believe or sense about a broader truth. Similarly, trust in societal terms needs to be incubated by patterns of expectation and behaviour.

The Contemporary Scene

A creeping suspicion of one another has been eating away at our sociality in all sorts of subtle ways in the last few years, as people have become increasingly polar-ised by competing identities: Brexiteer or Remainer, pro- or anti-lockdown, vaccinated or anti-vax, woke or cancelled. When ideological divides widen, empathy becomes harder to sustain, and as inequalities deepen, binaries become more brittle. Even proper structural attempts to address inequality can result in paralyses of trust on frontiers previously unrecognised. Twenty years ago, Onora O'Neill's now-famous Reith Lectures addressed a previous crisis in trust from a philosophical perspective, and in particular its relation to the media.[1] All these questions are essential to consider if we are to work towards a society in which human flourishing and wider environmental sustainability can become central priorities, rather than niche interests or useful slogans.

This essay began life as a lecture. When the series was first discussed, the title my colleagues suggested for my contribution was *Trust in the People*. This is clearly an immensely important topic in a representative democracy, not least at a time when that democracy is not quite as healthy as it should be. But it's not unproblematic, and I suggest that the problem lies in the definite article. Seemingly innocuous refrains such as 'the will of the people', alongside deeply chilling phrases such as 'the enemies of the people', set one group against another and raise the question of who may *not* be included in the phrase 'the people'. The American philosopher Judith Butler prompted us to ask who is missed out in the formula 'we, the people', which famously opens the Preamble to the United States Constitution. Any sense that 'the people' is a kind of amorphous mass risks undermining the dynamics of trust that can truly enrich society.

Scripture offers some salutary lessons here. For centuries, the Church's relationship with the Jewish people was characterised by what became known as the 'teaching of contempt'. This was rooted in the notion that the Jews had been unfaithful to God's covenant and were Christ killers. The resulting implication for Jews was centuries of persecution and exclusion across the globe, characterised by pogroms, genocide, and vicious anti-Semitic fake news and conspiracies that continue to this day. Some have argued that the root of this hatred can be found in the use of the phrase *hoi iudaioi* (the Jews) in the New Testament, particularly in the gospels of Matthew and John, where it is used frequently as a pejorative term, particularly (but not solely) in material around their accounts of Jesus's crucifixion. Similarly, the phrase *hoi ethnoi* is used across the New Testament and the Septuagint (the Greek translation of much of the Hebrew Bible), with a particularly negative tone. *Hoi ethnoi* is frequently translated as 'the gentiles', but it essentially means 'the others' – those who are outside the covenant, the unclean, the unfaithful. Again, it is often deployed in a pejorative way, referring to an amorphous mass of diverse people, defined simply by what they are *not*. Establishing who 'the people' are, how we describe them, relate to them, is a project that demands serious care.

In order to begin to rethink what 'trust in *the* people' might mean, in a world where cultural diversity within national boundaries is increasing rather than decreasing, and where the building blocks of public trust have been seriously corroded, we may need to think again both about the dynamics of trust itself, and about how we approach the subject of groups that either ask for trust or seek to trust.

The Dynamics of Trust

Trust is primarily a relational and moral reality rather than a legal one, even if elements of trust can be codified, systematised, mastered, even incentivised. If trust is really to be trust, it must spring from an active decision rather than a passive, or naïve, acceptance of a fait accompli. In his book *The Habit of Excellence: Why British Army Leadership Works*, Langley Sharp reflects on the Archbishop of Canterbury's view that 'if you don't care for your people, you can't ask them to do hard things.'[2] It is, of course, possible for people and groups to be falsely lured into *misplaced* trust – my colleague Anthony Ball describes in his essay how the current statistics suggest that trust is greater in oppressive regimes than it is in secular democracies.[3] But perhaps here we should differentiate, as he does, between cognitive and affective trust. Affective trust (largely an emotional or heart-based thing) is too easily abused, whilst cognitive trust (worked out in the mind and intellect) can be too easily incentivised. Perhaps what we are after in public life is a combination of the two, heart and head together, leading us to make decisions based on the reality or quality of the subject which is to be trusted.

Research published in the *Journal of Business Ethics* claims that ethical leadership leads to higher levels of both affective and cognitive trust. To be precise, in data harvested from 184 employees and their supervisors, this research claims that ethical leadership leads to the development of cognitive trust, which *subsequently* influences the development of affective trust.[4] In other words, in the professional environment it seems that people first engage in professional trust, before allowing a more personal element to enter the equation. But in this context, what might be the secret ingredients of that ethical leadership which lead to cognitive trust, and which open the way to affective trust? There will doubtless be lists of virtues, or people management skills, reflections on body language and group dynamics that can help here. But I was very struck by another anecdote offered in Sharp's book that perhaps offers the right kind of advice in distilled form. Patrick Marriott, the former commandant of Sandhurst, recalls asking cadets shortlisted for the Sword of Honour accolade four questions, which included, 'What have you learned of leadership?' He recounts that the best answer he ever heard was, 'To sacrifice control in order to command.'[5] This memorable line is followed by Sharp's reflections on the empowerment of individuals and groups within a clearly demonstrated command chain. Here is a profound example of a professional situation where the dynamics of trust really can thrive. Trust is a bond that needs to be strengthened and maintained from both ends of the relationship. Proving oneself to be trustworthy is a good foundation for being trusted – at least in the cognitive mode. But one notable thing about the Sandhurst cadet's answer is that there is a sense here of a leader giving something up, or relinquishing that which she or he may have held as an easier or faster option. It may be more straightforward, more reliable, more reportable, less risky to control a situation – but to command, to oversee, that needs responsibility, character, and (fundamentally) a sense of the whole operation. As Sharp goes on to reflect, for this to work well, it relies on empowerment of others, trust in their initiative, and openness when dealing with problems. In short, this is a mode of operation in which affective trust can really grow, because it shows trust in other people's character.

The Fact of Living

But why should we trust at all? And, in particular, why might the human person or human groups need to learn how to trust? The first president of the Czech Republic, Václav Havel, spoke of the 'tension between the living experience of meaning on the one hand, and its unknowableness on the other'.[6] He was not the first phil-osophical thinker to articulate this dialectic. Although the question is an ancient one, it is fair to say that the challenge has become more intense given the sheer amount of knowledge we now have at our fingertips. The more we know about the world, and our place within it, the more there is to know and – if we have any degree of humility and integrity – the more we realise we do not understand. In Havel's terms, the 'unknowableness' of meaning has become more complex – my own lived experience, with its accumulated narratives and tenta-tive working conclusions, is *only* my lived experience. In order to acquire any broader sense of truth and diverse complexity, I need to look beyond myself.

The Greek theologian John Zizioulas, who died in February 2023, did some of the most important work on personhood in the last half-century, and a brief study of some of his insights might help us develop a sense of why trust in people and trust in *the* people can share similar dynamics. Personhood indicates a degree of inherent dignity, a social identity, a network of relationships.

Zizioulas' groundbreaking first study was a book called *Being as Communion*, in which he explores the deepest meaning of personhood from the perspective of the Greek Fathers, the early and influential theolo-gians and writers in the Christian Church. His own exploration of the concept of personhood leads to some profoundly perceptive insights into the nature of the Church, but they can also help us in our task of understanding what a person is, and how that can relate to *people* in groups. Zizioulas begins with a study of personhood drawn from ancient Graeco-Roman cultures. From a Platonic perspective, a *person* in our sense of the word was ontologically impossible, because the soul was not permanently united with the body (it could constitute another individuality, for example, by reincarnation). The term *prosopon* (person) is related to the concept of a mask in Greek theatre – it is the mask that determines character, and through which the character works out his or her freedom and rationality. This 'person' is nothing but a mask, because man exists for the sake of the world, not the other way round. Hence the relationship of the actor with the mask is a tragic one, because it is only through the mask that the actor really becomes a person. Similarly in Roman thought, one may have social or legal relationships, indeed identities, collectively and individually, but these are not linked with the ontology (the inner nature) of the person. Roman thought, Zizioulas explains, is focussed on human reality as essentially forming associations or contracts, *collegia*, which organise human life in a society. Therefore, one individual can play very different roles – the Roman concept of personhood simultaneously denies and affirms human freedom: as *personae*, humans subordinate their freedom to the organised whole, whilst at the same time tasting the very tantalising possibility of freedom via this relationship to the state or *imperium*. It was this relationship that conferred selfhood and identity upon them.

In this climate, there is not any strong sense of personhood as identified with the being, inner reality, or dignity of the human. It was the outlook of the Bible, and the supple thinking of the Greek Fathers, Zizioulas claims, which united the person with his or her inner being and connected the person with an absolute sense of the self. Other contemporary theologians have articulated something similar. The American writer David Bentley Hart claims that Christianity's teaching about God taking on a human face in Christ changed our perception of the 'person' forever. I quote from his provocatively titled book *Atheist Delusions*:

In the light of Christianity's absolute law of charity, we came to see what formerly we could not: the autistic or Down syndrome or otherwise disabled child, for instance, for whom the world can remain a perpetual perplexity, which can too often cause pain but perhaps only vaguely and fleetingly charm or delight; the derelict or wretched or broken man or woman who has wasted his or her life away; the homeless, the utterly impoverished, the diseased, the mentally ill, the physically disabled; exiles, refugees; fugitives; even criminals and reprobates. To reject, turn away from, or kill any or all of them would be, in a very real sense, the most purely practical of impulses. To be able, however, to see in them not only something of worth but indeed something potentially godlike, to be cherished and adored, is the rarest and most enno-blingly unrealistic capacity ever bred within human souls.[7]

Zizioulas claims that such Christian insights are rooted not only in incarnation, but in faith in God not as a monolith but rather as a Trinity, where personhood *is* identified with relationship. There follows a compli-cated and slightly dense theological discourse, in which Zizioulas articulates that humans find it impossible to exercise their ontological freedom *absolutely*, because they are constrained by their 'createdness'. In other words, by the fact that they are not God. Humanity's inability to ensure its own absolute identity in the world culmi-nates in death, and yet Zizioulas argues that the person does not want simply 'to be' but rather 'to *exist* as a con-crete, unique and *unrepeatable* entity [my italics]'.[8] This cannot be assured by nature – the life of God, however, is realised as an expression of 'free communion, as love'. Zizioulas continues:

> Life and love are identified in the person: the person does not die only because it is loved and loves; outside the communion of love the person loses its uniqueness and becomes a being like other beings, a 'thing' without absolute identity and name, without a face … Life for the person means the survival of the uniqueness of its [inner reality], which is affirmed and maintained by love.[9]

As a theologian and bishop, John Zizioulas wrote about these topics from the perspective of one of the most distinguished Christian intellectuals of our age. We should note in passing that it is very difficult to discuss these topics of personhood and identity without venturing into the realm of religious language. But for now, I want to harvest some basic points:

1) It is possible in the twenty-first century to live in a way that locates our personhood only in the wearing of masks or the projection of roles. The personalities and images we frequently project via social media is one example of how widespread this temptation can be, especially

when our interaction with others is formulaic or fleeting. Furthermore, a focus on utility or 'usefulness' at the expense of appreciating deeper questions of identity undermine the possibility of trust, person to person.

2) One's identity and personhood is frequently subsumed into groupthink or the *collegia* system in much of the language and practice of twenty-first century democracies. We fail to take proper account of human dignity and fail to prioritise human flourishing when this happens.

3) Even the secular West struggles with the finitude of human existence, and still has a hunch that love is key to some kind of survival or existence beyond the grave, even if only in the form of cultural memory.

4) Being – personhood – is cultivated through relationships with other people. These relationships are founded upon solidarity and accountability. This is so between individuals, and I suggest these principles are also important for establishing trust between groups – trust that is simultaneously cognitive and affective.

Why Bother?

For John Zizioulas, the key theological word when discussing interpersonal relationships – in what can seem a disarmingly complex theological scheme – is quite straightforward. That word is 'love'. Reflecting on another great Eastern theologian, Maximus the Confessor, the writer Rowan Williams explains that this is a kind of dispassionate love, which does not engage on the grounds of individual characteristics, nor as a reward, but simply as the recognition of what all things are by their nature. This mutuality is 'To seek and to know the object *without self-referential desire* [my italics] ... and to love the unknown future' into which they are moving, 'to love the excess of their being'.[10] Such a scheme of relationship, to love others without subordinating them to one's own schemes and disordered desires, or subordinating them for one's own power or advantage alone, recognises others as 'excessive' and part of a whole that is impoverished without them.

Without this kind of relationship with others, humans are frequently collapsed in on themselves, self-referential and unable to truly recognise the other. In fact, the German reformer Martin Luther defined sin as a 'double turning-in-on-oneself' (*incurvatus in se*) – literally, turning inward so far that we cannot truly see around ourselves, see away from ourselves, or perhaps even see ourselves properly. Establishing how we relate to one another as *persons*, rather than as means to ends, is right at the heart of the question of how we establish trust. It is not only our neighbour who gains when love is a social force – we gain too, because our neighbour reveals a truth to us that we otherwise would not know. That might sound like rather a romantic thing to say, but it is primarily a statement about the limits of our own individual knowledge, and our need for one another to know anything more than a very partial truth in any given situation. In Sharp's book on army leadership, he reflects on the need for 'collective command' in situations that are simply too complex and intricate for one person to adjudicate without the expertise and advice of a wide range of others.[11] One general reflected that for this 'collective command' to work, a high degree of trust needs to be grown between teams and ranks, underpinned by 'good standard operating procedures as a handrail to speed, not a brake on initiative'.[12] This sense of dispassionate love, in which we relate to one another as persons, and as groups-of-persons, might yet be that cultural operating procedure.

As long ago as the 1990s, the commentator Harman Grisewood said that analysing contemporary culture was like trying to examine snowflakes in a blizzard. In the disastrously polarised debates of the last half decade, and in the hinterland of the culture wars that now threaten our common language and cultural grammar, we have begun to see how dangerous it is when we fail to appreciate and celebrate shared basic assumptions. We cannot imagine that it will be possible to strengthen trust between people, institutions, groups, or governments without some commonly celebrated basic operating procedures. In his essay, Anthony Ball highlights honesty, humility, compassion, and competence as four essential characteristics to underpin an improvement in public trust in institutions. In much of what remains of this essay, I want to explore just one quality that brings these themes together, and through which we may be able to deploy some of what I have suggested is important about personhood more broadly when considering questions of public trust.

From Dispassionate Love to Solidarity: A Handrail to Speed, Not a Brake on Initiative

Solidarity has been a particularly important tenet of Christian reflection on public ethics for well over a century.[13] It is one fundamental key in building trust between individuals, and also between groups. I want to root what I am going to say in two principles. First, the solidarity that operates within a market economy cannot always be described as genuine. If I am motivated by a certain outcome – a quid pro quo in return for my solidarity with you – this is unlikely to be mature or rich enough to sustain trust when challenged by flux or disagreement. *Gratuitous* solidarity is one that recognises the dignity of people or groups for their own sake, and not to gain something in return; it is enabled by empathy. The second principle is that we need to move away from the sense that solidarity only comes about when there is a common enemy. This is a particularly malevolent feature of contemporary groupthink. Solidarity can be weaponised, corrupted, but in those cases, it is unlikely to contribute either to the maintenance of genuine trust or be an adequate response to personhood. One might argue that the anti-Jewish movements inspired by that phrase *hoi iudaioi* were a form of solidarity – one group bolstering itself over another – but such solidarity was corrupted and unable to participate in a vision of love as a social and organisational force within the *polis*. True solidarity contributes towards the reinforcing or enriching of relationships.

In his encyclical *Fratelli Tutti* of 2020, Pope Francis offers the following observation:

The fragility of world systems in the face of the pandemic has demonstrated that not everything can be resolved by market freedom. It has also shown that, in addition to recovering a sound political life that is not subject to the dictates of finance, 'we must put human dignity back at the centre and on that pillar build the alternative social structures we need'.[14]

There has been a tendency amongst some philo-sophical and theological thinkers to dismiss the market wholesale, as if complete replacement of the system is currently possible, and indeed worth the assumption that the alternatives would be better. Rather than capi-talism in itself, however, it is neoliberal tendencies that fail to place human dignity at the centre of the conversa-tion, and which mitigate against trust. Indeed, genuine solidarity is something that is both necessary and pos-sible *within* the market itself.

Pope Francis continues:

Without internal forms of solidarity and mutual trust, the market cannot completely fulfil its proper economic function. And today this trust has ceased to exist ... In some closed and monochrome eco-nomic approaches, for example, there seems to be no place for popular movements that unite the unemployed, temporary and informal workers and many others who do not easily find a place in exist-ing structures. Yet those movements manage various forms of popular economy and of community production. What is needed is a model of social, political and economic participation 'that can include popular movements and invigorate local, national and international governing structures with that torrent of moral energy that springs from including the excluded in the building of a common destiny', while also ensuring that 'these experiences of solidarity which grow up from below, from the subsoil of the planet – can come together, be more coordinated, keep on meeting one another'.[15]

Pope Francis is arguing for the development of structures of trust supported by the principles of solidarity and subsidiarity. But he also suggests that social forms of friendship are at the centre of his vision. Experiences of solidarity need to 'keep meeting one another'. In other words, it is not sufficient for one or another group (no matter how rich in solidarity) to grow in a vacuum or to assume that such 'meeting one another' will happen by accident or osmosis. Instead, the task is to develop a new culture which takes seriously the many challenges of our age and places human dignity and the dignity of the good earth at the centre of the conversation. Towards the end of *Fratelli Tutti* there is a quite remarkable section where Pope Francis argues that encounter needs to become culture:

The word 'culture' points to something deeply embedded within a people, its most cherished convictions and its way of life. A people's 'culture' is more than an abstract idea. It has to do with their desires, their interests, and ultimately the way they live their lives. To speak of a 'culture of encounter' means that we, as a people, should be passionate about meeting others, seeking points of contact, building bridges … This becomes an aspiration and a style of life. The subject of this culture is the people, not simply one part of society that would pacify the rest with the help of professional and media resources.[16]

Not a vision of utopia, but rather a series of practices that demand hard work, strategic drive, and a willingness to face up to the reality of genuine difference and hard disagreement. Recognising that we need to create a climate in which it just might be possible to trust those with whom we may disagree would signify a deeply profound change in culture. As Pope Francis points out, this is not to argue for 'a consensus on paper or a transient peace for a contented minority'.[17] To trust across ideological divides, or between people and groups that come to rather different conclusions, is instead to risk a deep form of solidarity that under-tunnels the noise of a zero-sum culture, and enables trust to grow in ways that might not be immediately obvious. Rowan Williams calls this a 'contemplative' practice of politics, which works towards the difficult common ground on which the majority and the minority can negotiate together, instead of majority victories annihilating the hopes or commitments of a minority.[18]

Such a vision is liberated from the need to obliterate a common enemy to shore up its cause. Itself open to risk, rejection, and reconciliation, it takes seriously the fact that no single person or group possesses the entire truth. As Rowan Williams has put it, 'I can only be where I "truly" am by recognising that there is no fixed place where I am innocently and timelessly alone and incorrupt.'[19] We need to learn to trust wisely and discerningly whilst rooted in some fundamental virtues and values, in order to learn more about the whole world. We will only be able to sense the transformative power of trust when that process is supported by a whole architecture of virtue, when we are publicly able to gather around commonly held first principles that embrace and include rather than binarise or exclude.

In order for this to have any traction, we will need to take responsibility for our decisions, in the knowledge that people – including ourselves – frequently get things wrong. A culture of encounter is one where forgiveness, compromise, and reconciliation are not dirty words.

What could be more generative of trust than a fulsome apology? What is more human, more embodied, more revealing of a mature character – of personhood?

Conclusion

Towards the beginning of this essay, I shared my nervousness about that phrase 'trust in *the* people', principally because it has the effect of encouraging us to consider groups as amorphous masses, flattening out diversity, and leading to an unsustainable binary where some are 'in' and others are 'out'. I suggest that a theological description of personhood opens up a more attractive and appropriate vision, one which takes dignity, diversity, and relationship as primary characteristics that can assist in building the very trust we seek. Groups are groups of *people*, plural, and we need a rehumanising of our groupthink. So, instead of focussing on trust in the people, or indeed trust in people, perhaps we need to consciously work a little harder at building trust *within* the people. Solidarity – or, in theological terms, communion – depends on otherness, and it may be that the great crisis is trust amongst or within the people, and that is why our cultural sinews seem to be coming apart. Currently, even the obvious spaces for developing trust within the people are corrupted by less trusting logics – the Church falls into partisan lines; local politics is too often taken over by ideology. Social media, which could be a place where diverse opinions can be shared, frequently just shores up the tribe. And the creeping practice of online anonymity is especially destructive to the culture of encounter of which Pope Francis writes.

If we ever speak of trust in *the* people, or risk phrases such as 'the will of the people', we should take care to remember that 'the people' are in fact groups of *persons*, who therefore have multiple personalities and agendas, even when a single slogan threatens to obscure that reality. How they and we interact together, how we incubate trust, solidarity, and truthfulness as habits which do not need to be defended against 'another', are some of the greatest challenges of our age. To see our society as rich with the possibility of encounter amongst groups of friends might yet be a bottom line worth fighting for.

The Roots of Trust: Theological and Political Reflections on Trust In Troubled Times

Anna Rowlands

You who will emerge again from the flood
In which we have gone under
Think
When you speak of our faults
Of the dark times
Which you have escaped.

For we went, changing countries more often than our
    shoes
Through the wars of the classes, despairing
When there was injustice only, and no indignation.

 And yet we know:
Hatred, even of meanness
Makes you ugly.
Anger, even at injustice
Makes your voice hoarse. Oh, we

Who wanted to prepare the land for friendliness
Could not ourselves be friendly.

 You, however, when the time comes
When mankind is a helper unto mankind
Think on us
With forbearance.[1]

In 1968 the social philosopher and sometime critic of
Christian social thought Hannah Arendt published a
book in homage to this poem from Bertolt Brecht. She
titled her book *Men in Dark Times*, with each chapter
devoted to an individual Arendt judged to have lived
a life of substance. Such a life, she contended, had the
power to illuminate the darkness via its capacity to serve
the good: to struggle for justice in an unjust world, and
to do so in such a way that the person does not grow
harsh, deepening rather than losing their humanity in
the course of the struggle.

In the introduction to her book, Arendt writes:

Even in the darkest of times we have the right to
expect some illumination, and that such illumination
may come less from theories and concepts than from
the uncertain, flickering, and often weak light that
some men and women, in their lives and works, will

kindle under almost all circumstances and shed over the time-span that was given them on earth.

Arendt writes in dialogue with Brecht for two main reasons. The first is her belief that each generation lives through dark times, and the challenge is less to argue grumblingly whose times are darkest than it is to find ways to name and resist darkness: to learn what it is 'to live well the time on earth which was given me'. The second is her trenchant insistence that the thing that offers most genuine illumination is not concepts or cleverness (although so much of Arendt's work was precisely about the conditions for thinking well) but lives that are able to take into themselves the conditions of the world and, in their flickering uncertainty, walk a path that contradicts the darkness. These witnesses are the deepest bearers of hope, those who represent good faith and understand the call not only to create trust, but to embody *entrustment* – those who understand that we are bound to each other.[2]

To be clear, Arendt does not conflate 'living well' with living perfectly, or innocently, or blamelessly. She believes we must risk acting, with judgement, and bearing responsibility, and this means that we will not live innocently. Living well takes us via the mysterious pathway of human frailty, limitation, misrecognition, and failure.

Arendt is sceptical of those who present themselves to us as 'living well' because they are seen as 'mouthpieces of the zeitgeist' or 'representatives of the era'. Instead, she suggests that we gain more hope, more sanity, more courage from the lives of those who allow themselves to be troubled by their times and who find ways to make the times their own, struggling towards solidarity in whatever small way they can. Faith and trust in any given age emerge for Arendt through the lives of those who learn how to risk action, with others, towards building a common world. To live well, as we shall explore further on in this essay, is to venture, entrusted and entrusting, which is not simply to blindly trust. This mutual entrustment originates in the belief that we are bound together by particular kinds of promises.

A secular concern with the question of trust has become increasingly prominent over the last two decades (with, of course, an ecclesial/religious corollary – but addressing that is another story for another day). This public debate centres on a perceived crisis of social, political, and economic trust. The fear is that we are living with a collective experience of what we might call bad faith.

There are reasons to think that we *do* have *some* problems with trust and with faith: our times are increasingly polarised, with people viewing each other as either friends or enemies; trust risks being increasingly defined and exchanged based on a shared world view rather than given and exchanged on the basis of proximity, sheer interdependence, or, in the case of government or public bodies, perceptions of competence. However, researchers of trust are divided about the extent to which they think trust really *is*, in more objective and measurable terms, in crisis. Social theorist Russell Hardin suggests that to understand our crisis of trust we need to distinguish between two different kinds of relationship: interpersonal relationships – the kind where we expect forms of dignified reciprocal exchange – for example, those promises of reciprocity that ground trust between parent and child, partners, family members, and friends; and public relationships, in which we do not have reciprocal exchange in the same way. Hardin argues that even if we do not fundamentally trust the politician whose ideology we disagree with, we still have the right to hope for their basic competence. We expect a basic promise of competence and dependability, of judgement and responsibility from public servants, even those with whom we disagree. Hardin believes that we do not face an interpersonal crisis of trust – the trust that forms socially between, for example, friends, family, colleagues, and persons with shared interests and hobbies – because the only way to proceed sanely in the world is to find other individuals to trust. We go on trusting people because *we must*, in order to survive. Rather, what is being eroded continually in the contemporary moment is public trust: in the common goods that form through everyday practices in public institutions.

In her writings on politics, Hannah Arendt addresses the question of truth-telling and trust-building in politics. Arendt believes that truth and politics have never, in fact, been easy bedfellows. Lies, she argues, have *always* been deeply powerful ways for people to gain political advancement. If we are brutally honest, Arendt says, we will admit that truth-telling in politics has been the preserve of the political outsider more often than the insider. The truthful outsider is the whistle-blower who loses their insider status; or the Jeremiah-figure, crying out at the city gates to the derision and horror of his fellow citizens; or Socrates, wary even of writing his truth down, ultimately condemned to death. Political exile has been the historical fate of many a deep truth-teller – this is often not an especially attractive or comfortable place to be.

To be clear, such a view did not represent dangerous political cynicism on Arendt's part. No one believed more firmly than she in the value of active citizenship and politics, in its necessity, fragility, and virtue. Arendt thought our lives depended on it: in her own case even bodily survival, having fled the Nazis and remained stateless for over a decade. The same experiences had taught her that truth-telling in politics was not simple. Reflecting on this, Arendt's biographer Samantha Rose Hill argues that the question we should ask is not 'Why don't all politicians just tell the truth?' but rather something like 'What is happening at a deeper level in our culture when we suddenly start worrying publicly about the state of truth-telling and trust in politics?'[3] The most concerning reality is when systematic and organised deception or widespread disregard for public trust takes root at the heart of political cultures. Arendt believed that organised deception robs us, or uproots us, from reality itself, and you cannot be free if you are denied the conditions of knowing your own reality. On this point, it is a shame Arendt herself did not apply this insight more fully to the history of racism and the experience of Black communities.

Writing about our context now, Hill uses Arendt's works on trust and truth to argue that the reason we care about truth (in politics) is partly because we've lost much else. She notes: 'We've lost the ability to speak with ease, we've lost the ability to take opinions for granted; we've lost faith in science and experts, we've lost faith in our political institutions, and we've lost faith in democracy itself.'[4]

We are seemingly struggling with the possibility of a common world, or, expressed differently, *how we venture to create* a world in common. This is a problem that, by definition, belongs to us all. Of course, what the various movements challenging racial, gendered, environmental, and sexual discriminations of our age have pointed out is that this dilemma is hardly new, and its history is complex. There was no golden age of a common world that we simply lost. Arendt's point is made also with a consciousness that for stateless persons and refugees (of whom she was one) rights could only be honoured with citizenship, and without real political membership there is no properly common world for such people. Our age is one of loss of innocence, but also one in which many did not have the privilege of innocence in the first place. This loss of innocence relates to questions of race (colonialism), of class, of gender and sexuality, and of pervasive forms of social violence in institutions and families. Whilst the history that cultivated that veil of innocence should trouble us, its loss should not, for innocence is not what Arendt, or I, think we should be primarily seeking. Nonetheless, we live now with the question about what to do, and with few spaces in which to negotiate the answers together.

Arendt notes astutely that most people tend to think about truth and trust not in the abstract but in relation to the particular. Our need to anchor trust and truth in this way often gives itself away in our choice to speak of truth through spatial metaphors: we express truth 'in terms of something in proximity, distance and nearness; we approach and we depart from truth; "come close to it" or say that "nothing could be farther from it".[5] Hill notes that ultimately for Arendt telling the truth is meaningful in relation to the anchor points of a common world. Truth, as something that transcends personal experience or perspective, is difficult to invoke when we feel our common realm of existence to be fragmenting.[6] For Arendt, recognising the truth of 'something in particular' requires some sort of space of encounter and meeting: where I am able to appear in the world to you and you to me, and it is possible to share perceptions of our experience – even if we do not agree, because we don't necessarily need to agree to have a common world. Places of mutual encounter, in which we can sift together what is real and what is happening to us, is what forms the possibility of a common ground to stand on and gives us a sense that our reality has some kind of common fabric to it, and some real future possibility of either conservation or change. To this end, Arendt writes that political judgement is not primarily a matter of knowledge. Truth-telling is ineffective if it happens from nowhere; it is incarnated within time, place, relationship. Truth and trust are intimately related, like an ecosystem, and they are related to the particular conditions of one's individual life and our shared lives.

This is one of the reasons Arendt is so concerned with organised and systematic forms of deception and distortion, and the unreality they create. Shared, creative attention to reality is the condition of good politics. Anything that distorts that reality through deliberate misinformation or hiddenness makes that reality harder to know and is a serious problem for us. If we cannot face what is real, we cannot be truly free. Our unfreedom comes not by the act of lying alone, but by its distortion of reality. By distorting the reality of the present, we prejudice the future. This is not a closed, fatalist, or pre-determined position in relation to the future, but a warning of the temporal dimensions of our failures in the present.

Arendt's analysis finds interesting echoes in Onora O'Neill's 2002 Reith Lectures on trust. O'Neill notes that whilst she was sceptical of a hysterical 'there's no trust left' narrative, she is deeply concerned about the grounds on which it is possible to make safe judgements about truth and therefore sustain trust. Her diagnosis is that we are not a culture of total distrust but rather of mutual suspicion. Our bind is that although we are deeply suspicious, we are creatures who cannot stop placing trust. It is how we negotiate our everyday worlds with sanity; we have no option but to still place trust. But when much around us feels as if it's in ruins, it is difficult to do so with good faith. In the event, we continue to place trust but don't much believe in trustworthiness. This is an unhealthy spiral, in which we struggle to tell claims from counterclaims, truth from rumour, but we still need to discover reality and place ourselves in it somehow. Simply declaring that we have a crisis of trust and that we need more and better trust is, then, a blunt analysis.

In fact, for O'Neill it is precisely this idea – that a crisis of trust can be overcome by a rush to place more trust – that has led us astray. She clarifies that what we need is *better grounds* for '*reasonably placed trust*': 'If we are to place trust with assurance we need to know what we are asked to believe or accept, and who is soliciting our trust.'[7] Her considered and sharp question is: what are the reasonable grounds to place trust now?

O'Neill thinks that we began to head in the wrong direction in trying to answer this question around the mid-nineties. We thought we could fix public life with calls for a flood of public information, for data that would give greater openness and transparency – what we might see as society built like a computer (not her analogy, but a fitting one). 'This high road' back to trust, she says, 'is built on new technologies that are ideal for achieving transparency and openness.'[8] The paradox we face is that this seems to have done little to advance public trust, which has in fact 'receded as transparency has advanced'. Again, like Arendt, O'Neill notes that trust is not necessarily linked to transparency at all. Humans are, after all, not particularly like computers. We don't just need more information programming into our social systems. We are relational, social creatures, formed for relationships of promise and reciprocity, drawn towards ends and goals. Information alone does not float our trust boat, nor enable it to weather stormy seas. O'Neill points out that, from family relationships to doctor–patient relationships, our human relations are based more on mutual confidence than simply maximum information. Confidence that enables us to *act*, to claim our own freedom and use it *well*. What, then, builds that confidence?

We seem to live now with the paradox that we are in receipt of so much information to the point that we cannot absorb it, and yet live also with a level of deception and deliberate misinformation that was probably unimaginable when O'Neill's Reith Lectures were written twenty years ago. This is not, of course, an argument to say secrecy is good – it isn't – but it is an argument to say that 'if we want to restore trust we need to reduce deception and lies rather than [mere] secrecy'.[9]

O'Neill echoes Arendt's sense that what is most pernicious and to be resisted absolutely is the 'de-realising' qualities of deception.

Why so? Because, as O'Neill notes, active, organised deception creates deep inequalities between people – the deceiver does not treat the deceived as a moral equal: the deceiver distorts the capacity of the other to know and therefore to act freely. O'Neill is measured, however, in her reading of the effect of such deception: the perception of constant public deception results above all in a culture of suspicion in which we claim *not* to trust, but practically still must place trust, often in the very sources we have said we do not trust. I detest the values of Meta, Facebook as-was, and do not trust the platform, but still occasionally use Facebook because, in an age of hypermobility, this is how I can easily keep in contact with my many cousins and friends from childhood whom I no longer encounter much in person. I am a prime example of someone caught up in a culture of suspicion, yet who still ventures trust through habitual action. O'Neill concluded her lectures with the call, 'If we want to avoid this unfortunate spiral we need to think less about accountability through micromanagement and central control and more about good governance, less about transparency and more about limiting deception.'[10]

Hannah Arendt's interest was in something beyond

the historical instance of Nazism itself. She wrote to understand how societies lose their way and public and civic cultures become degraded. Her great political fear was the organised deception of whole societies by a particular group, class, or nation. Many feel that we live now increasingly with such forms of deception. This distrust teaches us to fear others and view them as enemies; it also creates individual distrust between citizens, which stops us from organising and discovering common interests across our differences.

I have sought to read the writings of Arendt and O'Neill as they might relate to our current moment, the world we share right now, in order to probe the question of how trust in particular operates in our society – trust in what, and in whom, and on what basis – and to question what the conditions are for sound shared judgements and shared actions. What are the conditions that shape the promise of the future, and the possibility of mutual entrustment? And this is where our question is, for me, theological.

So what, then, does Christian belief and practice have to contribute to furthering this conversation about human freedom in a common world? In one sense the answer is quite stark and simple: in the face of a modern drift towards detached scepticism, in which we must still somehow venture some trust to survive, but often feel conflicted as we do so, Christianity teaches the opposite – that health, both personal and societal, comes from a logic of attachment, of personalisation, and of mutual entrustment. The question is less 'should I trust you and you me?' and more 'to whom am I entrusted and who is entrusted to me?'. This is the heart of the first question that God poses to humanity in the scriptures, after the second great fracture of humanity: Cain, where is your brother? This is not an innocent question. It is still the dynamic at the very foot of the cross: as Christ's very body breaks under torture, he binds Mary, Jesus' mother, and John, the beloved disciple, to mutual care for each other: he entrusts them to each other, saying that John is now to become as a son to Mary, and Mary as a mother to John.

In exploring a little of this territory, we will find that we do not move far from some of Arendt and O'Neill's core insights – rather that we need to drill down into them.

St Augustine writes of the nature of Christian belief understood three ways: firstly, faith means believing God to be God; secondly, faith means believing what God says – believing the content of faith; finally, it means believing in such a way that the content of faith, and the life of God, becomes the goal of our life.

Belief for Augustine is in no sense abstract – it is

personal, directional, embedded. It is belief *in something in particular*: a reality, a particular set of events and stories we can find a home within. It is good faith in walking a particular path, one we wager will bring us towards love, towards delight, towards one another.

In his book on the creeds, Nicholas Lash writes beautifully of this tradition and what it teaches us about truth and by implication about trust from a Christian perspective.[11] He carefully translates the 'I believe' of the creed as closer to a statement of 'I promise'. It is 'I promise' rather than merely 'I know' or 'I assent to the opinion that....'. Lash argues that the 'I believe' of the creed is closer to the vow we make to a spouse than a curt statement of fact. It represents – as we pray it aloud – our consent to a particular way of living well and of loving well. And to state it in this way is to see the creed emerging from a complex chain of historical entrustment. In a meaningful and important way, we become the latest part of that chain of entrustment. Like a vow, it is a promise that we make without guarantee and with some risk and trepidation, but one we hope to grow into more fully over time, even if sometimes painfully as well as joyfully. In this sense, the life of faith is quite simply the enactment of promise, and a process of entrustment – and it is risk-laden, fragile, and vulnerable. John Henry Newman expresses similar thoughts about the life of faith when he argues that the best word to capture what faith is is 'venturing'.

Lash writes that to 'trust in God is to set our life, our mind, our heart, in God's direction'.[12] It is to establish our direction of travel and the horizon of our gaze, and risk choosing a path. It is to reject bad faith of every kind. But this is not to be taken to imply any direction we choose. The direction of our venturing is along the path walked by Christ, recounted in the stories of the scripture we are invited not just to read but to inhabit as the stories of the Christians before us, and also in the path-guide that is the Spirit, who gives us gifts that still our fear and strengthen us in the venture.

C. S. Lewis, in his writings on miracles, says something similar – that trust in the truth of the Triune God is personal from beginning to end, and this is its scandal and its disturbance in our lives. Lewis writes that it is always shocking to meet life where we thought we were alone.

'Look out!' we cry, 'it's alive.' ... An 'impersonal God' – well and good. A subjective God of beauty, truth, and goodness, inside our own heads – better still. A formless life-force surging through us, a vast power which we can tap – best of all. But God Himself, alive, pulling at the other end of the cord, perhaps approaching at infinite speed, the hunter, king, husband – that is quite another matter ... There comes a moment when people who have been dabbling in religion suddenly draw back. Supposing we really found God? Worse still, supposing God had found us? So, it is a sort of Rubicon. One goes across or not. But if one does there is no manner of security against miracles. One may be in for anything.[13]

Lash makes the helpful observation that this credal path of Christian faith is doubly educating. In the first instance it educates us in what and who is worthy of our time, attention, and love: what has dignity, value, beauty. The answer is God and neighbour – with a priority for the most vulnerable and discarded, including creation itself. In the second instance, it educates us in what we ought *not* to love: idols and false gods, including the spirits that taunt and trick us towards bad faith in ourselves and in our neighbours. Learning to believe in God, to trust in God, is learning to see value in something the way God does. In this sense, believing in God, trusting in God, opens us up to healthy and life-giving processes of entrustment. This trust is never blind, always particular, always ventured in the light of a promise we have chosen to put our trust in and receiving the trust that is put in us.

Trust in God, then, happens through engagement

with all that is most real in our lives. This is where we will meet God and find our neighbours. It is exactly the opposite of the processes of derealisation that encourages detachment, distance, disowning, or indifference, which drive mass suspicion and cynicism. In this sense, what is good for faith happens also (not by chance, the believer would argue) to be good for society. Faith is not a flight from the real but an unflinching attention to it, in community with others. Good faith is civic virtue too. Although it will be unsettling to civic authorities if they too are not able to risk acting in the light of human and ecological entrustment. Genuine civic virtue is always perceived as an outright threat and is starved of oxygen by regimes focussed only on the narrow private gains of small groups or individuals (a point St Thomas Aquinas makes well). It is also worth noting as an aside that where 'bad faith' occurs in the scriptures is generally where the community fails to hold its nerve under strained conditions, to believe and trust specifically in the promises of God, and to act with the conviction of mutual entrustment.

Our credal human believing is, Lash helps us see, our own version of frail and wobbly promising, a little akin to the flickering light that Arendt noted. But God's promise to us, which starts the chain of promising and makes our trust possible is, of course, of a different kind. Our promises and God's promises are not symmetrical. We break ours and must venture again, hopefully wiser but still fragile. Christ, as he was hanged on a cross, continued to stretch out bleeding arms to renew entrustment. The good news is that we cannot negate the covenant. We are mere creatures, not gods. And this is what makes hope possible in dark times – our only power is to receive forgiveness, to venture and begin again in the ruins.

St Paul portrays Abraham as the figural type of trust in God: placed under considerable strain and in struggle, he hopes against hope that things will be well because he trusts in God's promise, even when it seems insane to do so. Abraham's trust in the promise of God prefigures what Christ will do – the Truth in the form of a man, utterly particular and concrete, renewing the keeping of a promise. Not from ease but with arms outstretched he draws us into a common world and a shared future. Christ invites us to proximity, to draw near, to touch his wounds, and to tend to the wounds of each other. There is little security about where this might take us and whom it will draw us towards. Our response to that promise is sustained by the Spirit, through whom we are confirmed and strengthened in the face of what can seem a daunting task. The Church is formed out of this promise, sustained by this Spirit, and bears this responsibility from generation to generation.

Key scriptural texts, drawn upon by the early Church, that meditated on social trust enacted as a way of life included Matthew 25, the Beatitudes, and the Pauline texts. These texts teach the common good as utterly concrete and practical: feeding the hungry, clothing the naked, visiting the prisoner, welcoming the stranger, comforting the afflicted and grieving, weeping with those who weep, rejoicing with those who rejoice; building up the common body in its strength and vitality. But those same early Church communities were schools of faith learning not just how to hold people in common, but how to hold material goods in common. The common good and social trust are built in contexts where all have access to basic goods to meet common needs and the goods of creation are distributed fairly. Thus, questions about the just structuring of institutions and just access to basic goods are core to scriptural and early-Church visions of entrustment – the conditions for healthy entrustment are structural as well as personal.

In *Fratelli Tutti*, published in 2020, Pope Francis devotes a whole chapter to his interpretation of the Good Samaritan.[14] He reads the passage in the tradition of Martin Luther King Jr and Ivan Illich. All three interpreters emphasise the Good Samaritan's capacity to be so moved by the world that he is willing to leave behind his security as he confronts an urgent reality. Pope Francis argues that the scripture passage opens with a spiritually anxious question asked of Jesus, 'Who is my neighbour?' – who deserves to be part of my common world, my circle of trust, and who can I legitimately *not feel* responsible for? Francis wagers that Jesus' answer shatters that anxiety by turning the very orientation of the question – your neighbour is all whom you encounter to whom you have opportunity to become neighbour. This means there is the call of proximity – those we already know we are entrusted to and with – but also no fixed limit, no closed circle, no final border or boundary to a community. Sometimes totally unexpected events dictate whom we shall become neighbour to. Neighbourliness is a calling towards an expanding horizon within time and place, and it cannot be foreclosed. In this way, Christians are called to be the extension of the enfleshment and entrustment of Christ in the world, without end. Endlessly Christ stands amidst disaster entrusting us again to each other. If this sounds a bit sentimental it is worth remembering that in fact much of our modern way of living over several hundred years pulls us up from precisely these realities of entrustment; from time and place, from landscape and contingency. As Willie James Jennings argues, we have been encouraged by modernity into a logic of 'flying solo' – above land, time, flesh, place. Detached. Individuals. Sceptics. Minimally entrusting.

As Jennings implies, this is surely a crucial part of how we got race, gender, class, our relationship to land and other creatures so badly wrong.

In this sense, the trust trajectory that O'Neill and Arendt note is not the invention of the last fifty years, but an intense problem of the longer period of modernity. Here we stand, diffident, with a temptation to detach, yet still having to risk trust. Was this not the central dynamic of Thomas Hobbes' *Leviathan*? His answer to this anthropological diffidence, which he believed characterised our nature, was that we ought to create a centralising power in this temporal realm to overawe us. This is how we would manage our diffidence and create an artifice of mutual trust: a covenant from below creating a power from above that would result in trust brokered between us. The theological logic of the Good Samaritan, of St Paul, and of Abraham is different. The wounded social body is drawn together again, amidst failure, through multiple loving acts of committed entrustment. These acts are structural: renewed relationships must be formed so that our common resources meet the common material needs of all – there is no real action of entrustment without this. They are also personal: we are given to each other for more than mere need and distribution, but above all for the communion formed in reciprocal living. We are made for joy, not mere survival. Forging a way along this resurrecting social path is, like the Jericho road, an insecure route because it goes via the cross. But for the Christian it is probably the only route of good faith.

Notes

Trust in Oneself *by Claire Gilbert*

1   William Shakespeare, *Measure for Measure*, Act I, sc. iv.
2   Shakespeare, Act III, sc. ii.
3   Shakespeare, Act I, sc. i.
4   Shakespeare, Act I, sc. iv.
5   Shakespeare, Act II, sc. ii.
6   Shakespeare, Act II, sc. i.
7   Shakespeare, Act III, sc. ii.
8   Shakespeare, Act I, sc. i.
9   Shakespeare, Act I, sc. iv.
10 Yuval Levin, 'The Changing Face of Social Breakdown', *The Dispatch* (16 November 2021), accessed online.
11 Shakespeare, Act V, sc. i.
12 Shakespeare, Act II, sc. ii.

Trust In Institutions *by Anthony Ball*

1   Jonathan Perry, *Trust in Public Institutions: Trends and Implications for Economic Security*. New York:

United Nations Department of Economic and
Social Affairs, June 2021, 1.

2   Joanna Chataway, *Rebuilding a Resilient Britain:
Trust in Public Institutions*. London: Areas of
Research Interest, 2020, 7.

3   Organisation for Economic Co-operation and
Development (OECD), *OECD Guidelines on
Measuring Trust*. Paris: OECD, 2017.

4   Emanuele Sapienza, *Trust in Public Institutions:
A conceptual framework and insights for improved
governance programming*. Oslo: United Nations
Development Programme, August 2021, 7.

5   Institute for Public Policy Research, 'Revealed:
Trust in Politicians at Lowest Level on Record',
Institute for Public Policy Research (5 December
2021), accessed online.

6   '2022 Edelman Trust Barometer: The Cycle of
Distrust', *Edelman* (2022), accessed online 1 March
2022.

7   Richard Edelman, 'Breaking the Vicious Cycle
of Distrust', *Edelman* (18 January 2022), accessed
online 1 March 2022.

8   Kirsty Graham, 'Defaulting Back to Trust',
Edelman (18 January 2022), accessed online.

9   Perry, 2.

10   *Ibid.*, 2.

11 Valerie Frey, David Nguyen, and Sarah Hermanutz, *Building Trust to Reinforce Democracy*. Paris: OECD, 2022.

12 Perry, 1.

13 'Secretary-General Highlights "Trust Deficit" amid Rising Global Turbulence, in Remarks to Security Council Debate on "Upholding United Nations Charter"', *United Nations Meetings Coverage and Press Releases* (9 January 2020), accessed online 1 March 2022.

14 Sapienza, 9.

15 *Ibid.*, 8.

16 Bruce Chew, Michael Flynn, Georgina Black, and Rajiv Gupta, 'Sustaining Public Trust in Government' (London: Deloitte, 2021), *Deloitte Insights* (4 March 2021), accessed online 2 March 2022.

17 Margaret Levi, 'A State of Trust' in Braithwaite, A. Valerie and Margaret Levi, eds, *Trust and Governance* (New York, 1998), 88.

18 Matthew Bishop, 'Rebuilding Trust: What It Will Take', *Edelman* (2022), accessed online 2 March 2022.

19 Chataway, 8.

20 *Ibid.*

21   Simon Woolley, 'I Was an EHRC Commissioner.
     It Needs to Start Taking Racism Seriously', *The
     Guardian* (1 August 2020), accessed 10 March
     2022.

22   MORI Social Research Institute, *Exploring
     Trust in Public Institutions, Report for the Audit
     Commission* (London: MORI, 2003), 4.

23   OECD, *Drivers of Trust in Public Institutions in
     Finland*. Paris: OECD Publishing, 2021.

Trust in People *by James Hawkey*

1   Onora O'Neill, *A Question of Trust* (Cambridge,
    2002).

2   Langley Sharp, *The Habit of Excellence: Why
    British Army Leadership Works* (London, 2021), 42.

3   Jonathan Perry, *Trust in Public Institutions: Trends
    and Implications for Economic Security*. New York:
    United Nations Department of Economic and
    Social Affairs, June 2021.

4   A. Newman, K. Kiazad, Q. Miao, and B. Cooper,
    'Examining the Cognitive and Affective Trust-
    based Mechanisms Underlying the Relationship
    Between Ethical Leadership and Organisational
    Citizenship: A Case of the Head Leading the
    Heart?', *Journal of Business Ethics*, 123/1 (2014),
    113–23.

5   Sharp, 132.

6   Václav Havel, *Letters to Olga*, tr. Paul Wilson
    (London, 1990), 152.

7   David Bentley Hart, *Atheist Delusions: The
    Christian Revolution and Its Fashionable Enemies*,
    (New Haven, 2010), 214.

8   John Zizioulas, *Being as Communion* (New York:
    St Vladimir's Seminary Press, 1997), 46.

9   Zizioulas, 48–9.

10 Rowan Williams, *Looking East in Winter:
    Contemporary Thought and the Eastern Christian
    Tradition* (London, 2021), 53.

11 Sharp, 230.

12 Sharp, 231.

13 Pope Leo XIII's encyclical *Rerum Novarum* (1891)
    is frequently cited as a watershed moment in the
    modern unfolding of this tradition. Pope Leo
    writes of 'friendship', rather than solidarity per
    se, when exploring the condition of industrial
    workers, and the social and political contexts of
    labour. Successive popes have built upon these
    insights and developed them, up to and including
    Pope Francis, particularly in his *Laudato Si'* (2015)
    and *Fratelli Tutti* (2020).

14 Pope Francis, *Fratelli Tutti* (Rome, 2020),
    168. Pope Francis quotes his own 'Address to

Participants in the World Meeting of Popular Movements' (28 October 2014), 858.

15 *Ibid.*, 169.

16 *Ibid.*, 216. For further reading in this area, see Adrian Pabst, ed, *The Crisis of Global Capitalism: Pope Benedict's Social Encyclical and the Future of Political Economy* (Eugene, Oregon, 2011) and John Hughes, 'Integralism and Gift Exchange in the Anglican Social Tradition, or Avoiding Niebuhr in Ecclesiastical Drag' in *Graced Life: The Writings of John Hughes*, ed Matthew Bullimore (London, 2016), 148–60.

17 Pope Francis, 217.

18 Williams, 192.

19 *Ibid.*

The Roots of Trust *by Anna Rowlands*

1 Part 3 of 'To Those Born After', Bertolt Brecht, *The Collected Poems of Bertolt Brecht*, Tom Kuhn and David Constantine trans and eds (New York, 2018).

2 I have worked with an idea of entrustment woven from my reading of Arendt, Simone Weil, Onora O'Neill, and James Harvey's writing on dignity, combined with research findings from our Refugee Hosts project in the Middle East 2017–22 (www.

refugeehosts.org.uk). I am indebted here to each of these individuals and groups.

3   Samantha Rose Hill, 'Hannah Arendt and the Politics of Truth', *Open Democracy* (25 October 2020).

4   *Ibid.*

5   Hannah Arendt, *The Origins of Totalitarianism,* quoted in Hill.

6   *Ibid.*

7   *Ibid.*, 66.

8   *Ibid.*, 66.

9   *Ibid.*, 70.

10   Onora O'Neill, *A Question of Trust: The BBC Reith Lectures* (Cambridge, 2002).

11   Nicholas Lash, *Believing Three Ways in One God* (South Bend, Indiana, 1993).

12   *Ibid.*

13   C.S. Lewis, *Miracles: How God Intervenes in Human Affairs* (London, 1947), 94.

14   Pope Francis, *Fratelli Tutti* (Rome: Libreria Editrice Vaticana, 2020).

Westminster Abbey Institute

Trust in Public Life is published in partnership with Westminster Abbey Institute. Westminster Abbey Institute was established in 2013 to nurture and revitalise moral and spiritual values in public life, inspire the vocation to public service in those working in Westminster and Whitehall, identify and defend what is morally healthy in their institutions, and promote wider understanding of public service. The institute draws on Westminster Abbey's resources of spirituality and scholarship, rooted in its Christian tradition and long history as a place of quiet reflection on Parliament Square.